Culture.Shift

Creative Leadership for Audience-Centric Performing Arts Organisations

A Theatron Toolkit

for Strategic Audience Development

Editor: Benita Lipps

With the support of the Culture
2007-2013 Programme of the
European Union

Culture.Shift: Creative Leadership for Audience-Centric Performing Arts Organisations
A Theatron Toolkit for Strategic Audience Development
Editor **Benita Lipps**
Copy Editor **Nick Amies**

Copyright © 2015 Theatron[1]

Text Copyright © 2015 by the authors; by Nick Amies as author of all contributions not otherwise acknowledged

Image and Photo Copyright © 2015 by the organisations and authors as mentioned in the individual articles

ISBN: 978-0-9576843-9-3
First Edition: 1 July 2015
Lipps-Amies Publishing

Published with the support of the of the Culture 2007-2013 Programme of the European Union[2]

[2] The European Commission support for the production of this publication does not constitute an endorsement of the contents which reflects the views only of the authors, and the Commission cannot be held responsible for any use which may be made of the information contained therein.

www.culture-shift.eu

Table of Contents

Benita Lipps

Welcome to Culture.Shift!

This publication aims to be a practical, hands-on guide to strategic audience development. Rather than providing a concise academic review of the subject or a political analysis of the importance of audiences, 'Culture.Shift' is a collection of insights, tips and best practice examples.

This book is a guide created by creative leaders for their peers – hoping to pass on some of the ideas and experiences that proved useful. It builds on the work of the Theatron Network[1] – a 'EU-ropean'[II] collaboration of major performing arts houses to jointly develop new and better ways of engaging audiences.

This publication originated from the Culture.Shift Forum, held in Antwerp in December 2014. Many of the contributions reflect the programme and discussions at the event. At the same time, this book introduces new voices, and gives existing experts the space to elaborate on their ideas. Rather than being the final word in the matter, it should be considered a work in progress – and a contribution towards a Europe-wide debate on strategic audience development and community engagement in the preforming arts.

We hope it will foster new exchanges, projects, workshops and fora which – in turn – will enrich the next edition of the Culture.Shift Workbook with more new case studies and even more expert insights.

HOW TO USE THIS WORKBOOK

This book aims to be a companion to creatives working in the preforming arts who are interested in developing their audiences and creating deeper connections to their communities. It wants to encourage and support creative leaders on the road to a more strategic approach to audience and community engagement. By presenting best practices of houses that have already had their 'Culture.Shift', the book wants to inspire others to follow their example.

The book is divided into three sections:

1. The Need for a Culture.Shift
2. How to do a Culture.Shift
3. Elements of a Culture.Shift

The first section - **Towards a Culture.Shift** – provides an introduction to strategic audience development. The reader will gain an overview of what we mean when talking about a 'Culture.Shift' and about becoming a (more) audience-centric organisation. It provides a range of arguments why such a shift is increasingly important – not just from an economic point of view, but also in terms of artistic excellence and socio-political mission. The section ends with a summary of the talks and discussions from Culture.Shift Forum held in Antwerp in December 2014, providing some inspiration on how to continue developing the field.

The second section – **How to do a Culture.Shift** – looks at the skills and capacities necessary to instigate and successfully manage a 'Culture.Shift' in performing arts organisations. Four experts share their insights on Culture.Shift skillsets: creating the right mindset, collecting evidence, developing a strategy and investing creative leadership.

The third section – **Elements of a Culture.Shift** – looks at important building blocks of strategic audience development: communication, community building, engagement, education, co-creation and the learning organisation. It does so by presenting case studies from leading European performing arts houses, hoping that these examples may inspire others to follow in their path.

JOINING THE CULTURE.SHIFT

The publishers of this book – the houses of the European Theatron Network – strongly believe in the importance of fostering a dialogue on strategic audience engagement between creatives in Europe. Since the foundation of the network, its members have openly shared their ideas and insights – leading to new collaborations and innovative artistic adaptations.

Theatron invites others to join and enrich this dialogue – by contributing to the Culture.Shift discussion and resources or by joining the Theatron network.

Connect with us:

Culture.Shift:
http://culture-shift.eu and get in touch via info@culture-shift.eu

Theatron:
http://www.theatron-network.eu/ and get in touch via info@theatron-network.eu or
https://www.facebook.com/TheTheatronNetwork

[I] see www.theatron-network.eu

[II] Theatron is co-financed by the Culture 2009-2013 programme, now 'Creative Europe' http://ec.europa.eu/programmes/creative-europe/

PART I

The Need for A Culture.Shift

Lars Seeberg, Theatron

A New Theatre for a New Public

Theatron means theatre in classic Greek but originally it means "the place from where you look" which is why we thought that Theatron – stressing the point of view of the spectator - would be an appropriate name for our five-year performing arts project which focuses on audience development.

So, why this interest in audiences?

My own inspiration comes from a report for the Danish Ministry for Culture on the future of performing arts in Denmark, which I was in charge of a couple of years ago. For me the most interesting – or, maybe more precisely, alarming – discovery that the report revealed was that attendances in the public theatres in Denmark had quite drastically declined by 30 % over the last 30 years

I wanted to know why this decline had occurred and how this could be changed. I wanted to know how the European public theatre could still have a future in a buyers' market where nothing can be taken for granted anymore in theatre, in all other art forms or in the media for that matter. The culture shift – tradition to new-ness/verbal to visual/ individual to social - is simply prevailing globally.

One of the visitors for the committee in charge of the report was Dragan Klaic, one of Europe's truly cosmopolitan theatre scholars, who inspired our work to great length.

His analysis of the situation and his recommendations for change can now be read in a book published after his all too early death in 2011. I think that everybody interested in the situation and challenges for public theatre in Europe should read this book thoroughly. It's called: "Resetting the stage - Public Theatre between the Market and Democracy".

Klaic includes a couple of important quotes in this book which deal with exactly the same issues we in Theatron face:

"Public theatre is about free enquiry in a democracy; commercial theatre is about making money in a mass leisure market. An audience in a subsidised theatre is a micro-community of citizens, engaged in deliberative democracy, whereas in commercial theatre it is a group of consumers paying to be amused."

"…theatre is evidently no longer the main public pastime it was in the big West European cities of the seven-teenth, eighteenth and nineteenth century. It has become a minority option, one of many, among which are consumption of high-quality digital cultural goods…"

So, on the one hand it is potentially important. On the other hand it is not really dominant!

But why, then, do people go to the theatre? According to Dragan Klaic it is primarily because of "social motivation" – they want to spend time with other people to go to the theatre!

Still it is a fairly small percentage of the European population which attends public theatres, namely the so-called "silver tsunami". The well-educated, well-off, white section of society. Not the young, not that many men and hardly any representatives of new, first or second generation Europeans.

According to Klaic this can only be changed by the so-called 4P approach:

- programming
- partnership
- personnel
- public outreach

And this is exactly what we intend to analyse and practise during the five year of our collaboration in Theatron.

Together the partners and associate partners represent a stronghold of European performing arts. We already work with the challenges touched upon before, but we want to do better through mutual inspiration and collaboration.

We intend to present best practices for the whole European landscape of the performing arts in:

- new artistic expressions for new audiences
- new ways of engagement and outreach
- new ways of optimizing the work inside the organizations
- new ways of opening up our building to the public all day
- new ways of communicating with both our known and unknown public
- new ways of making theatre important to the society through public service
- new ways of basing our responses on knowledge instead of assumptions

When we have succeeded in that we shall be able to live up to the substantial potential of public theatre, which – according to Dragan Klaic – is "(that) it can shape a critical look at the world – the big, wide world – and at its key challenges and threats, sharing its own experiences and insights with the domestic audience, pulling them away from complacency and oblivion that the commercial theatre regularly seeks to engineer."

This encapsulates beautifully the goal of Theatron.

Benita Lipps, Theatron

Going Audience-Centric

WHAT IS STRATEGIC AUDIENCE DEVELOPMENT?

As Theatron Director Lars Seeberg pointed out in his welcome message: strategic audience development is not just about 'bums on seats', sexy marketing campaigns or affordable ticket prices. It's a top-level decision that can change the way performing arts organisations produce, perform and operate. While this certainly sounds important – and possibly a little intimidating – it doesn't really help us understand how to go about embedding strategic audience development in performing arts organisations.

Anglo-Saxon models have dominated the public discussion on audiences, yet there are as many definitions as there are approaches to audience development in Europe – one of the beauties and beasts of this culturally rich continent. In order to embrace and explore this wealth of ideas, models and experiences, we need to agree on a common starting point. Within the Theatron Network, we are in the process of developing a joint understanding – a consensus of what strategic audience development means for our members. It is this understanding that the Culture.Shift Workbook aims to present, discuss and develop.

For the purpose of this debate, we therefore propose the following definition:

> **Strategic audience development** is the active and deliberate process of creating meaningful, long-term connections between people and an arts organisation. Strategic audience development goes beyond increasing visitor numbers, aiming to build community ownership, participation, relationships with, and support for the organisation, its programme and its people.
>
> As a top-level activity, strategic audience development is anchored in the organisation's identity, goals and priorities – having an impact on both creative and operational decision-making.

Strategic audience development includes three dimensions[1]:

- "broadening" audiences (attracting more audience members like those currently attending),
- "deepening" audiences (enriching the experience of participants), and
- "diversifying" audiences (bringing new groups into the fold).

Strategic audience development takes the efforts of the entire organisation, including but not limited to:

- different ways of developing, (co-)producing, curating and distributing content,
- new approaches to research, marketing and promotion, and
- tailored educational and outreach offerings to communicate ideas, engage communities, empower participants and co-create new aesthetics.

There are two important assumptions embedded in this definition that will inform the Culture.Shift debate and consequently the contributions in this publication:

Firstly, strategic audience development starts with the **leadership**. It is not the task of a single person or department, but a mind-set that has to be embraced by the entire organisation – first and foremost its creative leaders.

Secondly, strategic audience development treats audiences as **partners**. Rather than viewing audience members as silent and passive consumers, it treats them as able stakeholders, willing and proficient to co-author aesthetic meaning.

STRATEGIC AUDIENCE DEVELOPMENT: A FORGOTTEN TRADITION?

While this approach to audiences may sound challenging – or even revolutionary – to some, it is in fact rooted in the very history of the performing arts: In the birth place of theatre - classical Athens - the audience was considered a key stakeholder and sovereign entity in terms of measuring and evaluating performances.

Those attending the drama competition at the Theatre of Dionysus in Athens in 425 B.C.E. (the year that Oedipus Rex competed) saw plays commissioned and produced through civic mandate and performed mostly by amateur members of the community. At the end of the three-day competition, the audience was invited to vote for the best play through a panel of elected judges. As Lynne Conner explains: "It would be folly to assume that 15,000 or so audience members sat quietly all day, […] Instead, Athenians disagreed with playwrights and with each other over the aesthetic, social, and political issues embedded in the tragedies. The historical record shows that they were extremely vocal in their opinions during the performance and afterward in the on-going civic debate that followed."[II]

This tradition continues well into modern times: Whether we are looking at Greek festivals, Roman amphitheatres or the Elizabethan public theatres of Shakespeare's days, audiences always played a loud and proactive part in the experience. Indeed – as Conner points out – until the end of the nineteenth century, Western audiences of all economic classes and from a wide variety of places were expected to participate actively before, during, and after a performance.

Only with the emergence of stage lighting – moving the audience into complete darkness – and the 'sacralisation of the arts'[III] in the late 19th century was audience expression actively discouraged – effectively eliminating the auditorium as a political public space. It seems that one and a half centuries later, audiences are demanding to be put back in the light.

THE NEED FOR STRATEGIC AUDIENCE DEVELOPMENT

Why have audience demands and expectations changed in the last decades? And why is it becoming increasingly important for performing arts organisations to listen to their audiences? It seems like a range of factors are coming together to create an entirely different socio-economical environment for the performing arts in Europe. Together, these factors make it harder for performing arts organisations to attract audiences, public support and funding. In addition, they have changed leisure time and the way people prefer to spend it.

On the one hand, these factors endanger the financial viability of performing arts organisations. Balancing less income with raising overheads and production costs increasing with technological demands, needs for additional services and expensive infrastructures is a severe challenge for many. On the other hand, it questions their role within society, the very reason for their existence.

In the following paragraphs, we will look at some of these, and how they are expressed in the trends and numbers in Europe:

I) Changing Demographics

Due to an overall <u>ageing</u> Western population, core audiences are greying (or worse –dying) and young people are looking elsewhere for entertainment and engagement. Unsurprisingly, European 15-24 year-olds are most likely to give "lack of interest" as a reason for not seeing (more) ballet, dance performances or opera in the last 12 months: 60% of 15-24 year-olds stating this reason, compared with 48% or less in the other age groups, who are more likely to give 'lack of time' or costs as a reason for non-attendance.[IV] A bigger surprise may be that it is the older Europeans who go to the theatre least often: 25% of those aged 55 and over having done so at least once in the last year compared to 32% of 15-24 year-olds.[V] If there is a 'silver tsunami'[VI] hitting Europe, performing arts houses are certainly not benefitting from it.

Globalisation and migration are changing the socio-cultural makeup of entire cities, creating new challenges concerning audience diversity and inclusion. Since the 1990s, migration has been the most important factor influencing the size of the population in Europe – much more than natural population growth.[VII] 50.8 million European residents were born outside their country of residence on 2015 – almost two-thirds of these in non-European countries.[VIII] 2012 saw 3.4 million people immigrating to EU-27 countries – approximately half of those from non-European countries.[IX] Migrants are forming a group growing both in size and prominence that cannot – and should not – be ignored. While they are contributing a wealth of cultural experience, practices and preferences to an ever-diversifying society, it also means that performing arts organisation can no longer rely on a single coherent community and core audience.

II) Competition for Leisure Time

Whether it is television, digital services, sports events, gaming or commercial events, people have more choices than ever when it comes to spending their free time. It is no surprise that all cultural activities are experiencing increased competition for the public's attention. Indeed, in Europe today, the most common 'cultural activity' is watching or listening to a cultural programme on TV or radio: 72% of Europeans have done so at least once in the last twelve months. Unfortunately, this shift has happened at the expense of the performing arts: the least popular activity is going to see a ballet, dance performance or opera, with just 18% participation.[X]

III) Technological Advances

The digital revolution has created a myriad of new cultural products, channels and services. These are not only competing with traditional cultural offerings, but have changed the modes of consumption. The interactive possibilities of web 2.0 and 3.0 have created a new generation of 'prosumers', who are no longer happy to sit quietly in the dark, but demand to be actively engaged.

Communication technology also reduces the 'pull of place' – making it less important to be somewhere physically or to seek entertainment nearby. Over half of Europeans now use the Internet for cultural purposes, 30% doing so at least once a week.[XI] On the one hand, this 'shift to virtual' increases competition of local performing art houses, on the other hand, it provides an opportunity for building new 'remote' audiences using digital channels.

IV) Economic Recession

The economic recession of 2008-2009 led to significant subsidy cuts in all areas that benefit from public funding, including the arts. In addition, people have had <u>less disposable income</u> or less free time at their disposal, making the attendance of cultural events more of a challenge. Unsurprisingly, expense seems a major obstacle to going to the theatre in those European countries that suffered most from the recession with Greeks (40%), Hungarians (37%) and Bulgarian (27%) citing costs as the key obstacle to cultural participation. However, it would be too easy to simply blame the recession and hope for better days. Theatres won't be able to attract audiences simply by lowering ticket prices: most Europeans give 'lack of interest' as the main reason for not going to the theatre (the first answer given in 21 Member States).[XII]

V) Waning Arts Exposure & Arts Education

Several studies have shown a solid correlation between adult arts engagement and childhood exposure to the arts.[XIII] Yet in most European countries, the number of people who <u>actively perform cultural activities</u> in their spare time – such as learning an instrument or joining a theatre club – is decreasing. In addition, <u>school curricula</u> have been tightened and refocused on the 'core skills' required to compete in today's economy.

Theatre and dance are particularly affected: Of the 38% of EU citizens who were actively engaged in an artistic activity in the last year, the most popular activity was dancing (35%), followed by photography or filming (32%) and singing (29%). However, acting on the stage or in a film is a minority activity, involving just 7% of those actively engaged in artistic activities.[XIV]

Interestingly, there are a significant differences within Europe – with active participation in the arts decreasing drastically when moving from North-West to South-East Europe: 74% of Danes, 68% of Swedish, and 51% of the French indicated of being actively involved in cultural activities in the last year – compared to 14% of Bulgarians, 20% of Italians, 21% of Hungarians and 26% of Greeks and Romanians.[XV] These differences are mirrored in the attendance figures in these countries to a large extent.

VI) Change in political attitude

It has also been argued that the performing arts in Europe are facing a change in the political attitude to culture in general and cultural subsidies in particular. [XVI] The broad political consensus in Europe that quality art institutions deserve public subsidy for the public benefit they create has been slowly eroding since the economic recession. Instead, the performing arts are increasingly required to satisfy the type of (financial) performance indicators that are used when evaluating socio-economic investments. This shift is <u>changing the funding conditions</u> from artistic excellence to economic performance and contributions to solve societal challenges. Attracting (the right) audiences and serving one's community thus becomes increasingly important when applying for public funding.

VII) New Aesthetics & models of (co-)production

In addition to facing the external challenges to their existence, many performing arts organisations have an intrinsic, internal need to develop their audiences. It is a need that is as essential as it is straightforward "theatre without an audience is [simply] impossible".[XVII]

Developing new relationships with audiences brings more than money – it brings new creative challenges and aesthetic opportunities for the performing arts: To quote the findings of the 'Arts for All: Connecting to New Audiences' conference[XVIII]: "Along with the rest of society, arts groups are questioning some of their most fundamental assumptions about how cultural participation works: what motivates people to engage in certain leisure activities, what forms of creative expression capture the public's attention, how people learn about cultural events and how they fit art into more crowded lives." Incorporating demographic diversity, utilising technological advances and collaborating across cultural and national borders can inspire and enrich cultural productions – as we will see in many contributions of this publication.

A CASE FOR STRATEGIC AUDIENCE DEVELOPMENT

Society is changing and the performing arts – as both a mirror of and creative laboratory for society – has no choice but to change with it if it wishes to remain relevant. In the words of Dragan Klaic: "A ready-made audience does not exist. It needs to be continuously discovered, developed and fostered. Without a continuous educational engagement and demonstrated work on interculturalisation and inclusiveness, no performing art deserves public subsidy."[XIX]

To maintain the strong, healthy cultural life that Europe is known for and that our communities deserve, performing arts organisations need to get better at building demand, appreciation and passion for the arts. Strategic audience development – when rooted at the very core of the organisation and implemented through a broad range of activities including programming, outreach, communication, education and management – can help performing arts organisations to redefine their role and regain social and cultural relevance. This requires a shift in both thinking and doing – in philosophy and practice: a 'Culture.Shift'.

Is it worth the effort? The publishers of this publication – the Theatron Network members – would answer this with a whole-hearted 'yes'.

[I] the 3 dimensions are taken from the Wallace Foundation's publication 'Building Arts Organizations that Build Audiences' (2012)

[II] Lynne Connor: In and Out of the Dark. In Engaging Art: The Next Great Transformation of America's Cultural Life, co-edited by Steven Tepper and Bill Ivey (2008)

[III] Lawrence Levine: Highbrow/Lowbrow: The Emergence of Cultural Hierarchy in America

[IV] Special Eurobarometer 399 (2013): Cultural Access and Participation, p. 34

[V] ibid., p. 21

[VI] term coined by Dragan Klaic in 'Resetting the Stage' (2012)

[VII] European Foundation for the Improvement of Living and Working Conditions (2010): Demographic change and work in Europe, p.5

[VIII] numbers for 2013 from Eurostat (2014): Migration and migrant population statistics

[IX] ibid.

[X] Eurobarometer 399 (2013): Cultural Access and Participation, p. 5

[XI] ibid., p. 6

[XII] ibid., p.27

[XIII] see: Bob Harlow: The Road to Results (2014) and Eurobarometer 399 (2013): Cultural Access and Participation, p.54

[XIV] Eurobarometer 399 (2013): Cultural Access and Participation, p.51

[XV] ibid., p.50

[XVI] Dragan Klaic (2012): Resetting the Stage

[XVII] „...doch wie Theater ohne Publikum nicht möglich ist" – Friedrich Dürrenmatt: Theaterprobleme. In: Horst Turk (1992) Theater und Drama, p.172

[XVIII] The Wallace Foundation (2008): Arts for All. Connecting to New Audiences)

[XIX] Dragan Klaic (2012): Resetting the Stage

Erwin Jans, Toneelhuis Antwerp

A Living Conversation in a Wild Bar

TOWARDS A NEW 'ENGAGED AUTONOMY' IN THE (URBAN) PERFORMING

Ten years ago, under the revealing title How Much Globalization can We Bear? (2003), German philosopher Rudiger Safranski wrote a still relevant essay on the many confusions or "entanglements" associated with the process of globalisation. This notion of 'entanglement' is clearly expressed in the challenges of the 21st century city and its growing complexity: Today, more than half of the world's population lives in cities, and this number continues to grow. Cities exercise a huge attraction. At the same time, the urban challenges are gigantic. The Flemish writer Stefan Hertmans describes it like this: 'a deep humanitarian significance – one that may never be lost sight of – continues to cling to the concept of the city. The city is the territory of man-made communication par excellence, in its most advanced form.'

The arts too are developing more emphatically in relationship to this urban context: in the meantime terms and concepts such as audience participation, cultural diversity, education, social-artistic projects, ecological awareness, urban engagement, social participation, art in the public space, neighbourhood action ... have become an integral part of the vocabulary with which the arts reflect about themselves and their functioning.

FROM AUTONOMOUS TO NETWORKED ARTS – A PARADIGM SHIFT

It is no exaggeration to say that a paradigm shift is taking place in defining the place of the arts in society. Until now, this place was marked by autonomy. It is this notion that is in crisis at the beginning of the twenty-first century, or at least in need of redefinition. This crisis is closely linked to the crisis of two other forms of autonomy: that of the individual and that of the state. Nineteenth century civil culture was based on a dual development: that of the individual and that of the nation. There is undoubtedly a connection between the autonomous individual, the autonomous nation and autonomous art. The three notions emerged around the same time – the second quarter of the nineteenth century.

Free-floating art

In this social context of an assertive bourgeoisie and developing market capitalism, art emerges as an autonomous domain with its own rules of production, distribution and reception. It breaks away from all servitude to church, nobility or bourgeoisie, despite the fact that literature, art and music play an important role in the formation of national awareness at certain moments. Modern art is characterised by what we can call a form of 'social free-floatingness'. It is no longer associated with a specific worldview and is no longer supported by a clearly delineated religious, political or economic elite. It develops independently of institutionalised social expectations and cultural prohibitions. It shows little interest in the demand for intelligibility, beauty or entertainment. Moreover, it is highly self-reflective. In its avant-garde variant, modern art is provocative, subversive and shocking. This notion of autonomy has become the core of art's functioning since the early twentieth century.

We are the entanglement!

However, in the process of globalisation, the autonomy of the individual and of the nation state – the cornerstones of modernity – have been weakened and cut back. Both the individual and the nation, each at its own level, have been incorporated into a network of relationships. Which does not mean that they no longer exist or have become completely powerless, but rather that they function in a way that is radically different than before. The nation state no longer has its former sovereign power, and must share its power with transnational institutions and organisations.

Individuals have also become nodes in a network that includes not only our relationships with other people but also and mainly our embedding in or 'logging in to' a mediatised society. In a network society, the inter, the between, becomes more important than the intra, the inner. In this perspective, we above all are dividuals, 'two-seers', instead of individuals, a term that literally refers to our so-called indivisibility. Philosopher Henk Oosterling puts it as follows: 'We are entwined in networks. We are not entangled. We are the entanglement[1]. In my opinion, we have always been entangled. Entanglement is our human condition.' Oosterling states that the confusion and entanglement of the postmodern person, eagerly in search of strong stories instead of Great Stories, is bound by culture and time: 'The foundations of the oppositions between which the tightrope has been strung for 150 years, have been eroded. High and low in culture, right and left in politics, good and evil in morality, true and false in science have now finally become, like beautiful and ugly in art less than a century ago, empty terms. Quality presents itself elsewhere.' The contradictions at the foundation of modernity seem to have had their day.

It is obvious that the art world is also affected by this 'entanglement', this 'networking' of society. For some, the end of modern autonomous art is already almost a fact. For American historian Wendy Steiner, for example, the 20th century is the century of 'autonomous' art, which she calls 'sublime'. The 21st century on the other hand is for her the century of heteronomous art, which she associates with 'the beautiful'. In her vision, the sublime stands for wrenching, disturbing and alienating art that seeks no recognition from a specific audience or a specific community, while the beautiful stands for communication, consolation, openness and dialogue with the audience.

Unmeasure

However, (thankfully) things are not this simple and black & white. The point is not the contrast between subversive and affirmative art. It is important that art preserve its quality of being 'un-measure' (a term of Paolo Virno): a 'un-measure' that repeatedly questions and challenges the 'measure' of culture. However, it is important to interpret the 'un-measure' of art much more broadly than the provocative, subversive and nihilistic gesture of avant-garde art. It fundamentally concerns searching for a new relationship between art and society, where it is also crucial to make a distinction between the individual artist and the artistic institutions. Participation is broader than social-artistic and educational practices in the sense that it points to a broader trend within the arts to deal differently with their audiences and involve them more as active partners in the processes of creation and the production of meaning.

The comment of art critic Anna Tilroe brings us a little further. She asks for a revision of the notion of quality as well as the notion of art history: 'The discussion concerning what quality is and what quality has must be conducted more broadly and via a different approach. The art historical project initiated at the beginning of the twentieth century can no longer be considered as the only one. We need to acknowledge that multiple art histories exist and can be written about.' Tilroe pleas for greater openness and attention to developments taking place outside the art world, but also within art itself 'from the VJ and website culture to partnerships of artists, architects, designers, fashion designers, researchers and commercial undertakings'.

These new developments, together with the growing cultural and ethnic diversity in cities, force a repositioning of cultural and artistic practices. The evolution of media technology, commercialisation, the impact of popular culture, the demands for recognition of minority groups, the debate on participation... undeniably have an impact on art, the artist, art institutions and the experience of art.

BECOMING ENTANGLED/ENGAGED AUTONOMY – APPROACHES TO ARTS TRANSFORMATION

A raw, wild bar...

In his State of the Union at Het Theaterfestival 2009, Tim Etchells (Forced Entertainment) poetically appeals to the image of a new type of artistic institution: 'I think we need a theatre that, after it is broken, is only partially glued back together, by those who need it and in the manner that they wish. The unused pieces are left behind on the ground for those who can use them later, or for the early morning dustcart. It doesn't matter. We are not obliged to hold on to something that is no longer useful. We can best view it as a living conversation, a raw, wild bar ..., a street corner, as an opening in time and space, and not as a museum.'

Etchells' ideal is that of a theatre broken and broken open. In a poetic and metaphorical text full of summaries and juxtapositions, Etchells evokes the image of a theatre containing the space of all of life and precisely because of this is broken and fragmented. Fragments (of a history, of a tradition) that can be used freely by anyone who needs them. Continuous self-questioning, keen self-awareness, experiment, capriciousness, ambiguity, are the keywords of a theatre that is as agile as the world in which it is

established: 'Theatre that criticises its own language while still using it. Theatre that undoes its own rules, that lays bare its own authority. Theatre that divides its audience. Theatre that can also 'bring together' an audience, even when while criticising that expression and its meaning. Theatre that is constantly breaking out of its own boundaries, immersing itself in performances, installations, events, the void.' In short: Etchells gives theatre a very hybrid but generous interpretation. Theatre that is open to new impulses from within and from without, artistic as well as social.

Un-Art

In a lecture from 2007 How to Grow Possibility: The Potential Roles of Academies, Charles Esche, director of the Van Abbe Museum in Eindhoven, introduces the term 'engaged autonomy' to clarify his position on the autonomy issue: 'Engaged autonomy defines the necessity of an agonistic (as well as antagonistic) response to the issues at hand – be they economic, political, aesthetic or even curatorial. To this extent, engaged autonomy needs to be specific in its address – to a certain public, a certain condition, a certain geography or a certain interest group.

Artists would need to know to whom they want to show or speak, not to presume the old bourgeois public for lack of any other.' The artistic practice is about the creation of an authentic space for discussion (agonistic, but also antagonistic) in relationship to the important issues of our time. This is necessarily situated in time and space, and always addressed to a specific public. Esche here raises the idea of universal art and again localises it in a specific time and place.

Charles Esche goes one step further by detaching the term 'engaged autonomy' from the art object, and interactively linking its quality to the context and the viewer. Art in this way becomes a form of behaviour: 'For me, the term becomes even more interesting if it can help to map out a set of relationships between art and public that is less invested in the quality of objects but more in states of being and action. We could call this "Exchange" perhaps, or what Kaprow refers to as "Un-art". His idea of art as a behaviour that allows you to be self-critical, that permits you autonomy in relation to your context, that is held in your head and allows you to be an autonomous individual within the system.' Autonomy here shifts from a quality inherent in the work of art to the critical, autonomous attitude of the individual, among others and perhaps in the first place, of the individual spectator. What Esche here calls 'Exchange' is the core of what we understand by 'participation'.

7000 oak plants

This is in keeping with Joseph Beuys' erweiterter Kunstbegriff / broadened concept of art, which as-

sumes creativity as the basic dynamic for every conceivable society. For Beuys, art is at the heart of all human labour and each form of collective activity: law, economy, governance, education. One source of inspiration for Beuys was Rudolf Steiner, who viewed the experience of art – aesthetic contemplation – as a part of the social organism and as a lever for the development of freedom, equality and solidarity.

The concept soziale Plastik / social sculpture devised by Beuys summarises this link between social philosophy and art. A good example of this is his last great performance as artist during documenta 7 Kassel in 1982: the 7000 Eichen project. 7000 oak (and other trees) were planted between 1982 and 1987 in Kassel, and next to each oak, a pillar of basalt. Beuys planted the first oak; his widow and his son the last. Beuys initially encountered opposition from the Kassel petite bourgeoisie, but in the end, he succeeded – mainly via associations, neighbourhood committees and schools – in generating considerable enthusiasm for his project. Beuys aims to go further than Marcel Duchamp, who at the beginning of the 20th century, with the ready-made, launched the attack on a concept of art understood too institutionally. Beuys breaks free from the museum, and focuses on the anthropological possibilities of an expanded idea of creativity – an artistic approach to all material objects originating in the human mind. The work of someone like Benjamin Verdonck is close to this. The work of Thomas Bellinck with illegals is also a moment of 'soziale Plastik'. They are artistic practices that go in search of their own limits, and in so doing enrich and expand the notion of art.

Art as public space

The public urban space is a particular challenge for the artistic practice. It is the place par excellence where the conflicts and opportunities of the globalised world present themselves. The neighbourhoods and streets of the big cities are 'the contact zones' of the world, in which cultures and people who until now were separated by geography, history, race, ethnicity, etc. are forced to live together – always in the context of power and unequal relations – in the same space, and thus forced to engage in a form of translated relationship with one another.

Art lends itself to giving physical form to these translated relationships, but in this case the relationship between art and public space must be fundamentally reorganised. Henk Oosterling raises questions concerning the traditional interpretation of art in the public space: 'The old idea of art in the public space retains only a limited effect, partly because architecture has undergone such aestheticism, partly because the idea of a statue in the public space no longer squares with our hyper-mobile and layered experience of the space. (…) We need

to move from the notion of art in the public space to that of art of the public space and art as public space. Artists have the creative expertise to appropriately reflect social interactions in the public space.

You can also think of art as a public space in which the creative process and the participation of all stakeholders are central. The artist does not work towards a finished product, but considers as his or her material the creativity and inventiveness of, for example, the residents who make use of a specific public space. The artist puts the creative process in motion, but does not know in advance what the result will be. Even though there is indeed a commitment to realising a specific project.'

INTER-EST, RESET & PLAY: TOWARDS A NEW VISION FOR (URBAN) CULTURE

Where do the above ideas and examples lead? To a practice of art that is no longer alongside or opposite society, but rather is interwoven or networked with it. This applies both to the work of the individual artist and to the artistic institution. For both, the moment of autonomy – 'the unmeasure' – remains the point of departure, but there is already an openness at their core, the possibility for what Etchells calls 'a living conversation'. Concepts such as 'engaged autonomy', 'erweiterter Kunstbegriff' and 'art as public space' include the possibility to redefine artistic practice based on an idea of participation without (fully) abandoning the achievements of autonomy.

Assuming/Taking on Urban Inter-est

Henk Oosterling uses for this the term 'inter-est'('inter-esse': literally to 'be between') and defines it as 'self-interested involvement'. Interest as between-ness as well as active concern or participation. He prefers 'inter' to 'multi' (intercultural, interdisciplinary, interactive) because it emphasises the relational. When I use 'interest' here, it is with the same meaning as 'participation'.

An artistic practice characterised by 'interest' is involved with its social, urban, political, ecological, educational … context. Just like schools are increasingly developing into 'community schools', so too will artistic institutions need to become more 'communal', with greater interest for their surroundings.

Artistic institutions as well as individual artists must search ever more intensely for the 'invisible cities' within their city. This of course is a reference to Italo Calvino's book of the same name, in which Marco Polo describes to the Kublai Khan the same city – Venice – in dozens of ways. In the context of this article, the 'invisible cities' stand for those urban dimensions that often, all too often, are in danger of being missed by artistic

institutions: specific audiences that are not represented, specific neighbourhoods located beyond the artistic radius, specific practices that are not included in the programme, etc. But the (now still) 'invisible cities' also stand for the future of cities.

For artistic institutions, it might indeed be a good idea to draw maps at the level of the city or the region showing the underlying 'strings of interest'[II] . Where are the artistic, cultural, social and educational institutions and organisations located in an urban context? What are their relationships? How intense are these relationships? Where are the gaps? Where are the audiences that are never addressed? Where are the organisations that have never been contacted? Where are the schools that have little or no participation in artistic life? Reflecting on 'participation' ('interest') at urban or regional level cannot be done without such sociological analyses and sociological maps.

The realisation of being a node in a larger network also means involvement in the entire network and in the overarching responsibility for this network. Not every artistic institution in a city must take on the same duties and responsibilities. This can be negotiated. It is important that at urban or regional level, a 'living conversation' takes place between the different institutions and individual artists on their collective and mutual interests, on the strings that may or may not connect these institutions.

Resetting the stage

What would such a 'living conversation in a wild bar' actually look like? In his book Resetting the Stage, Dragan Klaic develops the practical aspects of the notions 'participation' or 'interest'. He calls upon the performing arts themselves to examine their programming, their communication, their advertising, their networking, their local integration, their public activity planning, their international ambitions, their artistic leadership, the composition of their boards of directors, etc. He calls for a critical and creative examination of all levels, recognising that innovation is possible and necessary everywhere.

In this exercise, the 'public' character of subsidised theatre must be the focus. In a leisure sector that has become much more complex and competitive than it was several decades ago, subsidised theatre more than ever must emphasise its uniqueness, its 'accessibility': its critical approach to the tradition, its continuous pursuit of innovation, its attention to experiment, its sensitivity to radical demographic and cultural shifts, its interest in all forms of verbal and non-verbal expression, its capacity to integrate new technological developments, its potential to communicate with the public in surprising ways, its community building power, its local and international networking, its artistic diversity and polyphonic character, etc.

Klaic suggests among others organising more in thematic clusters in order to make the abundance of what's available transparent to the public. Theatres must also organise their own 'mediatisation' and no longer be dependent on dwindling media attention. Each theatre must redefine itself based on its own history and its own local character. Dragan Klaic also points to the importance of focusing on a young audience, but also the importance of attention to an audience older than fifty that constitutes a large part of the population. They too can still play an important role. For him, the development of the arts is most deeply connected with the emancipatory processes in modern democracy, with the defence of the public space and public discussion, and with the opposition to global consumption and spiritual superficiality. Intimately associated with this is the idea of continual learning, for young people but also for adults. Art institutions provide a special context in which to organise ongoing learning (interest) in a non-dogmatic way.

Becoming cultural players

Inter-est primarily means living among unruly tensions. It involves frictions, interactions, surprises, encounters, reflections, etc. To describe our relationship to reality, Indian cultural critic Homi Bhabha uses the expression: 'beyond control, but not beyond accommodation'. We are no longer master of the game, but we do have play, in the sense of room to manoeuvre.

I purposely use the word 'play' here. The possibility to play might just be that which makes us human – the homo ludens of Huizinga. Playing is the possibility to open up the context and thus make possible a different game. Ultimately, it is about asking ourselves whether our capacity to play is enlarged. Culture is in principle this (room to) play. In it we shape our identity, our history, our future desires.

In our multicultural cities – 'the contact zones of the world' – we have more cultural players than ever before, with more histories, more stories, audiences, sensibilities, aesthetics, etc. Art is not militarising but socialising; it is not made for a public, but it creates a public. It is not up to art to launch a revolution as was still the case with the Avant garde, but to implement specific forms of 'conviviality'. Art creates a type of respite or breathing space, necessary conditions for any collective slowing down.

CONCLUSIONS

It is extremely important to create mental and physical (rooms to) play.

Breathing space. A clearing. Groups and individuals all too often remain 'out of play'. The artistic and cultural rules of the game are too often defined by the 'white' majority without taking into account the many minorities in search of a voice. Recovery of accessibility stands or falls with the creation of new places capable of giving cultural and artistic expression to the new urban reality and it's still untapped potential. These places are the material translation of an intercultural 'ethos'. Only then can we achieve a new vision of culture that does not see culture within ethnic lines, but as a radically unfinished social process of self-definition and transformation.

This article is a shortened version of the one written for the Vti (the Flemish Theatre Institute) in 2014.

[I] *Oosterling here makes use of a wordplay in Dutch involving 'in de knoop', to be entangled or confused, and a 'knoop' or a node in a network.*

[II] *Referring to the 'strings' of Ersilia described by Marco Polo: As material city, Ersilia has disappeared. What remains are innumerable colourful strings that are strung throughout the city, which indicate the relationships the people of Ersilia had with one another. In other words, the network of strings makes the 'inter-est' of Ersilia visible.*

Monica Urian de Sousa, European Commission

We Need Audiences, Audiences Need Us

The approach of Creative Europe, EU's programme for the cultural and creative sectors

In this article, I will explain the European Commission's vision of audience development and why audience development is a new priority in the Creative Europe programme. The article includes a discussion on trends in European cultural policy which accompany the work on this priority. It also refers to civil society's expectations of the European Commission, as well as open the way for a fruitful and continuous dialogue on this topic, which should be envisaged in a long term perspective.

We are in the process of a fast-paced paradigm shift in the European cultural world. Never before has the cultural offer been so rich – both in terms of quality and quantity, often despite cultural budget cuts that have affected many countries. Digital technologies have made it easier for a huge number of people from all across the globe not only to access culture, but also to create, share, curate and distribute cultural content as they wish. A large part of society is eager to be engaged in all areas of life – from democratic participation to crowd-funding, from environmental campaigns to social economy.

Moreover, the disappearance of borders inside the EU and the existing funding schemes at European level encourage – at least to a certain extent – the mobility of artists and works of art, thus the diversity of European culture can travel both physically and digitally much more easily than before. At the same time, competition from other leisure activities is fierce, both online and offline.

On another level, the rise of terrorism and extremism of all sorts, the democratic deficit manifested through apathy towards (or discontent with) political processes, as well as ever-growing poverty and social inequalities are questioning our model of society. And the list of challenges and opportunities goes on and on, making our epoch an uncertain and complex one, full of contradictions.

The issues at stake are not only social and economic, but also (and sometimes more importantly) symbolic and cultural. In this context, we are convinced that cultural participation has benefits for individuals at various levels (in terms of personal development, identity-building, creativity, and well-being), but also as a bridge-builder between people and between communities. It is thus relevant for us – both the European Commission, a public funder for arts and culture, and the cultural institutions themselves – to ask ourselves: how are Europeans navigating through this situation? How do they appreciate the enormous cultural wealth that this continent has to offer, which is seen from abroad with admiration and sometimes even with envy? What are the roles and the responsibilities of artists and cultural institutions in this landscape of permanent transformation? Culture can certainly offer many answers to these burning questions, but which is the most effective way to embrace it so that these answers are heard by the people who need them most? How can we consciously build a new society in which culture has a central role to play for individuals and for communities?

CULTURAL PARTICIPATION IN EUROPE

As a principle, ensuring that people enjoy richer, more fulfilling lives by taking part in cultural activities – a fundamental human right in the Universal Declaration of Human Rights – is a priority of the European Commission. This concern is shared by many other national, regional and local authorities, as well as by cultural institutions and artists worldwide.

Since both policy-making and cultural management should be based on a sound picture of reality, and have clear, measurable goals in order to succeed, it is essential to start by analysing Europeans' behaviour relating to arts and culture.

The Eurobarometer survey on cultural access and participation, undertaken in 2013 (comparable to the Eurobarometer survey on European cultural values in 2007), is probably the only survey that captures the reality of all the 28 EU Member States in one snapshot, according to consistent criteria and analysis.

The latest results were extremely worrying for a certain number of countries (particularly – but not only – in Southern and Eastern Europe). Overall we can see that cultural participation has declined in Europe over the last five years, across all traditional forms of arts and culture (except cinema), both actively (amateur arts), and passively (audience membership).

The two main reasons for not participating are lack of interest and lack of time. If we combine these data in an index of cultural practice, taking into account frequency of participation in various cultural activities, the picture that we get shows that a large proportion of Europeans either have no access at all or only rarely have access to any type of culture. Socio-demographic factors are still predicting participation in culture to a large extent, with people in more deprived circumstances (in terms of income and education level) participating to a much lesser extent than people with a higher education profile and higher incomes. In some cases these groups are not participating at all.

Furthermore, only small minorities of Europeans participate in cultural activities from another country (let alone in another country). Thus, European cultural diversity remains inaccessible for a large part of the population. National surveys have confirmed the same trend, signifying, to a certain extent, the failure of policies relating to access to culture/democratisation of culture implemented in many European countries.

Undoubtedly, the situation is too complex to be understood by statistics alone, as representative as they may be. The decrease in public funding for culture, the lack of artistic education curricula in schools, and the economic and financial crisis are just some of the causes that contribute to this seemingly helpless situation. The Directorate-General for Education and Culture in the European Commission has on several occasions advocated an increase in budgets dedicated to culture and education (particularly in times of crisis, when some of the national budgets for these areas were cut), and has highlighted the need to include artistic education in school curricula.

In any case, these phenomena pose a major problem in terms of the failure to use public funding in a redistributive way. Moreover, the role of culture as an agent for social transformation is being seriously undermined.

Nevertheless, we believe that there exists a space where cultural organisations can act directly, doing what it is within their power to improve cultural participation, a space where the European Commission can offer its support. This "space" is audience development.

AUDIENCE DEVELOPMENT

When we started working on this topic, we quickly realised that there was no universally accepted definition of audience development, particularly across different countries, since this English expression is not translatable in many languages. We decided to use the definition of the Australia Council for the Arts, which, being a generous one, matched our vision the closest: "Audience development is a strategic, dynamic and interactive process of making the arts accessible. It aims to engage individuals and communities in experiencing, enjoying, participating in and valuing the arts through various means" including arts marketing, volunteering, digital tools, co-creation and many others. An essential idea to keep in mind is that audience development is not an end in itself, but a process that involves the whole organisation, not only its management. It will not work if it is a top-down approach.

For the sake of clarity we distinguish be-tween:

- increasing audiences (attracting more people with the same socio-demographic profile);
- deepening relationships with audiences (encouraging repeated visits, discovery of related or even more complex art forms, fostering loyalty towards the institution)
- diversifying audiences (attracting people with a different profile from the current audiences, including the non-attenders or people without previous contact to the arts).

What would it take for a cultural organisation to adopt an audience-centric approach? This implies for many organisations a major change of attitude: the realisation that they are not the gate-keepers of culture anymore. The choice is between joining the conversation that the audiences are already having, and losing them altogether. It is a question as well of choosing to be relevant to the time and the space inside which an organisation acts. It is a search for meaning for the organisation in relation to itself; but also in relation to the human beings with whom it comes into contact and whose lives it wants to touch; to communities of different natures that it interacts with. This includes those people or communities who do not attend the organisation's activities, but who would be interested in doing so, as well as those who are totally excluded from cultural participation at the moment, but could benefit from it.

We can say that an organisation which is audience-centric (or in transition towards it) is sensitive to its environment, to its societal responsibility and long-term sustainability; it accepts that being relevant today has implications on cultural, social and economic levels.

Audience development can only be implemented successfully if the whole organisation is involved, from top management to security services, and cannot be confined to a specific department or team. Moreover, it requires various departments to step out of their silos and work together, in order to create synergies, share information and inspire each other. Nevertheless, cultural leaders are an essential driving force of this process of transformation (as in many other change processes).

CREATIVE EUROPE

The EU programme dedicated to the cultural and creative sectors, Creative Europe, was launched in 2014 for a period of 7 years with a budget of approximately €1, 5 billion. It covers all Member States of the European Union, the European Economic Area, the candidate and potential candidate countries (Western Balkans, Turkey, etc.), but it is also open to the countries of the Eastern and Southern Neighbourhood (such as Georgia, Moldova, etc.), depending on their signing agreements with the European Commission. To date, the programme covers 38 countries in total and this number is growing.

Audience development has been chosen as one of the priorities of the Creative Europe programme in order to cope with some of the challenges that were mentioned above. For the first time ever in the history of EU financial support to cultural operators, the demand side is given an equal footing to supply side. Other priorities of the programme are cross-border mobility, capacity building, digitisation, new business models, training and education.

Audience development is a specific objective for both for the Culture and the Media sub-programmes of the Creative Europe programme, which aim to:

- "reach new and enlarged audiences and improve access to cultural and creative works in the Union and beyond, with a particular focus on children, young people, people with disabilities and under-represented groups";
- "foster policy development, innovation, creativity, audience development and new business and management models through support for transnational policy cooperation".

The Culture sub-programme of Creative Europe works on the basis of calls for proposals and evaluations by independent experts. Different kinds of support are available: for cooperation projects; for cultural networks; for cultural platforms; and for literary translations. The approach to audience development plays an important role in assessing the quality of the projects and their contribution to the objectives and priorities of the programme.

Audience development is present in all these types of support:

- in calls for proposals dedicated to net-works or cooperation projects, improving audience development skills and capacity may be one of the aims of a project itself, or if these skills exist already, an audience development strategy can be one of the main activities of the project, accompanying its cross-border mobility or digitisation strategy. From the first call for proposals for cultural cooperation, we have seen that 60 out of the 64 projects selected in 2014 tackled the audience development priority in one way or another. This gives us a powerful signal that the culture sector has understood how important it is to seriously work on this topic.

- in calls for proposals for networks, plat-forms and literary translation, applications involving co-creations, co-productions, touring performances and translations should have a clear strategy for audience development to accompany the project and to ensure that the activities have the largest possible impact.

A DYNAMIC APPROACH

The visibility given by the Directorate-General Education and Culture (DG EAC) of the European Commission to this topic (during the conference "European Audiences: 2020 and beyond" in November 2012, the European Culture Forum in November 2013 and other high-level events) has given the culture sector the opportunity to exchange their experiences, to find international partners for projects and to advocate this topic in a more convincing way in their own countries. It is truly remarkable how much experience already exists in this field, and how many cultural organisations have already reflected upon this; however the knowledge is somewhat scattered across different countries and sectors, thus there is a need for a focal point to gather this information.

The announcement of this priority has created an enormous wave of interest that we are still feeling today. We have concrete proof that a number of national governments and funding bodies have followed the Commission's example. This has created a virtuous circle, since a larger number of cultural organisations who are committed to working on this topic are able to get funding for their projects at European, national, regional or local level; while the reflection on audience development is very much alive and it creates mutual inspiration for culture professionals.

This vision of the DG EAC is constantly evolving thanks to contact with the "real world", from listening to cultural operators who share their experience with us, to the projects that we support or people who inspire us.

One of the things we have realised, one year into the programme, is that the most difficult aspect is diversifying audiences without losing the existing ones. Diversification as a type of audience development is truly a challenging and long term project, which requires an in-depth revision of the way a cultural organisation works (including programming).

We launched a study on audience development from the point of view of the transition of a cultural organisation's structure towards a more audience-centric approach. Our aim with this study is to in-spire organisations to adopt this new way of thinking, and to help them by providing them with sound arguments to use in front of anyone they need to convince (internal or external stakeholders). We expect the results of this study in 2016.

An expert group will also be invited by the European Commission to discuss this topic in the context of the Creative Europe programme, to make sure that the audience development priority is well understood and well implemented.

RELATED CULTURAL POLICY DEVELOPMENTS

Hand in hand with the work done by the Creative Europe programme, work on this topic is ongoing in the cultural policy field, with the intention of encouraging policy and practice to be nourished by each other.

In previous years, the question of access to culture has already been tackled by the two main mechanisms managed by the DG EAC in the cultural policy area: the Open Method of Coordination (OMC) and the structured dialogue with the civil society.

The OMC is a voluntary process of dialogue between experts from the Member States, who share their experiences and learn from each other on a given topic. Previous topics have included promoting better access and wider participation in culture in public cultural institutions, and the role of cultural institutions in promoting diversity and intercultural dialogue.

On 25 November 2014, the Council adopted a four year Work Plan for Culture. This Work Plan focuses on four key priori-ties where acting at EU level can deliver a clear added value: accessible and inclusive culture; cultural heritage; cultural and creative sectors: creative economy and innovation; promotion of cultural diversity, culture in EU external relations and mobility. With regard to the priority area 'accessible and inclusive culture,' the Work Plan foresees the establishment of two Open Method of Coordination (OMC) working groups. The first OMC group has just started and will end in 2016. It will aim to promote access to culture via digital means, by identifying "the impact of the digital shift on audience development policies and the practices of cultural institutions", in a context where "digital technologies have changed the way people access, produce and use cultural content."

To do so, experts taking part in the OMC working group will "map existing policies and programmes and identify good practices", and produce a manual of good practice by the end of 2016.

In parallel to this, a structured dialogue with civil society on the same topic will feed into the debate and will try to answer the same questions, in a complementary way. Thus, civil society and the Member States have an equal voice and will work together to advance current thinking and approaches to the crucial topic of audiences and the digital shift.

CONCLUSIONS

First of all, the funding opportunities under the Creative Europe programme are there to be seized and we hope that the best projects working on audience development will be selected in the years to come.

DG EAC acts as a facilitator in the area of culture, and audience development is no different: the dialogue between the cultural sector, the Member States and the European Commission will continue to be, we hope, a fruitful one, with each partner respecting the knowledge and the motivations brought to the table by every other partner in this dialogue. You are of course invited to participate in this dialogue and share your ideas, concerns, success stories and failures with us.

DG EAC will also continue to champion this theme at the European level, on the one hand in an awareness-raising exercise and on the other hand by bringing the best projects under the spotlight, so that other cultural operators can learn from them.

There is one thing we can anticipate for sure: the process of change will continue in the cultural world at all levels. The better cultural actors are equipped to deal with this change and adapt to it, the more their audiences will become their loyal ambassadors. The courage that is needed to experiment with new forms of engagement, whilst keeping the high level of artistic quality reminds me of a quote in Peter Brook's The Devil is Boredom: "for something extraordinary to happen, an empty space must be created first". Let us create the best conditions for this empty space where artists, cultural organisations and audiences can really meet. We need each other.

REFERENCES AND FURTHER READING

[I] European Commission (accessed on 1 March 2015). **Eurobarometer on cultural access and participation 2013.** [webpage]. Available: http://ec.europa.eu/public_opinion/archives/eb_special_399_380_en.htm#399

[II] European Commission (accessed on 1 March 2015). **"Survey shows fall in cultural participation in Europe".** [webpage]. Available: http://europa.eu/rapid/press-release_IP-13-1023_en.htm

[III] European Commission (accessed on 1 March 2015). **Eurobarometer on cultural values 2007.** [pdf]. Available: http://ec.europa.eu/public_opinion/archives/ebs/ebs_278_en.pdf

[IV] European Commission (accessed on 1 March 2015). **Brochure European Audiences: 2020 and beyond.** [webpage]. Available: http://bookshop.europa.eu/en/european-audiences-pbNC3112683/

[V] European Commission (accessed on 1 March 2015). **Conference Report European Audiences: 2020 and beyond.** [webpage]. Available: http://ec.europa.eu/culture/library/reports/conference-audience_en.pdf

[VI] European Union (accessed on 1 March 2015). **Report on the Role of Public Arts and Cultural Institutions in the Promotion of cultural diversity and intercultural dialogue.** [pdf]. Available: http://ec.europa.eu/culture/library/reports/201405-omc-diversity-dialogue_en.pdf

[VII] European Union (accessed on 1 March 2015). **Report on Policies and good practices in the public arts and in cultural institutions to promote better access to and wider participation in culture**. [pdf]. Available: http://ec.europa.eu/culture/policy/strategic-framework/documents/omc-report-access-to-culture_en.pdf

[VIII] European Commission (accessed on 1 March 2015). Creative Europe Website. [Webpage]. Available: http://ec.europa.eu/programmes/creative-europe

[IX] P. Brook, Le diable c'est l'ennui, ed. Actes Sud, France, 1991

Meta Štular, Culturemaker Institute

The Culture Shift Forum 2014

On the 6th and the 7th of December 2014, the Culture Shift conference took place in the Toneelhuis in Antwerp. Organized by the Theatron Network, the forum sparked discussions between Europe's leading creative directors, experts in change management and audience engagement, and European creative leaders. 38 participants from eleven countries discussed good practices, strategies and tools needed to face important cultural and societal changes related to recent economical crisis and digital shift.

INSPIRING CREATIVE LEADERSHIP

The first part of the conference was dedicated to the presentation of best practice examples. Artistic directors of leading European performing arts organisations shared their leadership approach and strategies. They explained the logic behind their decisions, the challenges they have faced, the ways they have involved their teams and their communities, and what was the impact of their approach. **Lars Seeberg**, director the Theatron network, and the founder of see@rt, presented the objective of the conference - to find out how the theatre in Europe can survive and prospect in a situation when national subsidies are becoming increasingly modest. In his welcome speech he evocated the 4P approach - programming, partnership, personal and public outreach[1]

and stressed that theatres should engage in continuous effort in order to follow their mission.

A. Storytelling and openness

Jerry Aerts, General and Artistic Manager of the international arts campus deSingel, presented the challenge of fulfilling the 36000 m2 of space with content and audience. In pursuing this objective, they decided to connect grandeur and adventure. They wished to broaden their audiences and to do that they have employed different strategies. On one hand they have broadened the impact of the events by several accompanying activities aiming at specific audiences, and by engaging many partners from different fields. On the other hand, they have deepened the communication with the audiences by using the storytelling principle. He explained that this important principle is a two way process which enables in depth communication and underlines the importance of never closing the environments and leaving every activity wide open to the community. In order to get good stories, an organization should give people the possibility to tell stories about it in their own way. He presented a good example of media partnership consisting of professionals coaching young reporters. Those are youngsters who make short clips about the DeSingel events and are sharing them with their friends on social media. Thus, young audiences are reached in the most appropriate way - by their peers. Those are DeSingel ambassadors as well as youngsters who are fond of deSingel programming and who recommend the events to their friends at school by creating special school-specific advertisements and marketing approaches.

B. Non-commercial alongside commercial

In the beginning of the speech **Alistair Spalding**, Chief Executive and Artistic Director of Sadler's Wells, pointed out that, since its beginnings, the house sold water alongside performances. The business model of his institution was always based on combining commercial and artistic offers. With the goal of broadening the audiences of Sadler's Wells, they have focused on two objectives: to make a strong identity of a dance house and to make associate artists the centre of the new creative policies. By following those objectives, Sadler's Wells has doubled the audiences in last ten years. The speaker underlined that this shift was made possible by the fact that they also sell commercial performances along the artistic ones.

Another important fact is that the theatre applied direct marketing strategies to the artistic performances at Sadler's Wells. This also coincided with a digital shift, allowing the replacement of written promotional material by more attractive and direct video clips. To reach different communities and to broaden the audiences they have diversified their programming. They have introduced other festivals in the theatre programme, opened the doors to non-professional practices, and have introduced a ticketing system, which encourages spectators to buy a ticket for a performance they would not necessary go to see.

All these new practices have also resulted in crossover of audiences. To conclude, Alistair Spalding underlined the following key words: **clear identity, direct marketing, and high art alongside commercial performances.**

THE BENEFITS OF AUDIENCE-CENTRIC APPROACH

After the presentations of best practices, the participants focused on the following questions: Do you really need to engage your audiences in the creative process? How can this be done without compromising the artistic vision? Moderated by **Benita Lipps**, Coordinator of the Theatron Network and Director of the DaVinci Institute, a vivid debate took place, showing that the leaders of European theatres face complex challenges demanding dynamic, inclusive, and site-specific responses.

A. Digital shift and new ways to communicate

Lars Seeberg underlined that it is impossible to take any interest of audiences for granted. **Cultural professionals have to be better in explaining what kind of experience one can get in a theatre** compared to the variety of internet, TV and other digital content.

Erwin Jans, Dramaturg and Responsible for audience development at Toneelhuis, was of the opinion that the situation is similar all over Europe. Public space of today is much more influenced by visuals or by advertisement. Public space is becoming virtual; therefore we need a new definition of it. He pointed out that the art community had failed to explain why art has changed so much. They expected that audiences would follow, which did not happen. In his experience, **creating environments where audiences get closer to the artists is rewarding for both**.

Jerry Aerts described how deSingel is today partly a database

and partly an arts organization. They have more than 300 videos, innumerable forum comments, and amateur photos from students... He remains convinced that today **theatres have to add new content but they especially have to find new ways to communicate about that content**. The major concern should be how to get into society in much more various ways than just announcing a new performance.

B. Blurring the limits and new ways of collaboration

In Toneelhuis, they are opening the theatre to new audiences with direct approach via open rehearsals. **Erwin Jans** explained how this experience further involves some of the amateurs in professional performances. In this way, the limits between professionals and amateurs are being blurred. He evoked the philosopher Peter Sloterdijk, who said that Olympic point of view was not possible any more, since one is always in the midst of something. Therefore, we have to let ourselves be intoxicated by the world. We should try things and see what comes out of them. **Artists are nowadays in search of new ways of collaboration; they are searching for new audiences in open public spaces**. He underlined that public space plays an important role in creative commons.

Jerry Aerts concluded that the most important task of theatres these days is **the creation of a community that believes in something common.**

C. Lack of subsidies and market constraints

Erwin Jans was of the opinion that, since there are many constraints from the market or from the funders, the concept of autonomy in the arts is also changing and should be redefined.

Alistair Spalding explained how the situation in the United Kingdom is different from the rest of Europe. **The British were more ready for the recent shift since they did not get the notion of a citizen paying for the arts from his taxes.** The tradition of commercial theatre has existed since Shakespeare.

Jerry Aerts gave an example of how the specific dance and theatre scene developed in Flanders in the 1980's out of a lack of national subsidies. Given a difficult financial situation, the companies had to search for funding internationally. Suddenly, they became a part of an international repertoire. With this success, national interest and subsidies started to rise. With the current shift, **Flanders organizations have the advantage of having succeeded the generation of artists and companies who made it**. Their artists gave them pride and self-confidence to become more entrepreneurial.

Meta Štular, founder of Culturemaker Institute, asked the panelists to elaborate on the lack of public subsidies. In her opinion **public subsidies represent public interest and translate public values.** She reasoned that we are getting too easily used to the situation of making culture without public subsidies and that it seems as if we are preparing to accept the idea of the market principles penetrating the world of arts.

D. New theatre network and knowledge exchange

In **Lars Seeberg's** opinion it completely makes sense to make a new theatre network today. The proof is that in two years of the Theatron project, the repertory and the outreach of two Danish theatres have changed. He hoped that the Flanders model would be copied - **smaller companies in small countries should reach out to international audiences**. He explained his belief that theatres have to focus on what they are really good at. They have to try to create different channels towards audiences adapted to digital age.

Alistair Spalding did not think it was so easy to learn from other examples. He underlined that **we all have to work in our own contexts. It is not possible to apply the same practice to different circumstances.**

LEADING CREATIVE TRANSFORMATION

The second day of the conference focused on concrete plans for implementation. The leadership experts shared insights on the skills, tools, methods and processes needed in order to become an even more effective creative leader. They underlined that a successful changes should start with the right questions and with the right choice of people. Everybody should be involved - from administrators and artists to funders and communities.

A. Asking the right questions

Graham Devlin, Cultural Strategist & Former Deputy Secretary General, Arts Council of England, stipulated that first questions to the participants should be why one wishes to transform something. He explained that there are different drivers behind the transformation and he listed them: societal and economical changes, diversification of leisure options, the phenomenon of social networks, climate change in relation to touring, systemic change moving from the age of oil to the age of information. Therefore, it **is very important to identify the reasons for which an organisation wishes to change**. Given the scale of changes in last few years, cultural organizations have become more creative in adapting to changes. He stipulated that in this process, **art organizations have to be art-centred and audience-focused**. He continued by presenting another set of questions that cultural organisations should ask when considering change. Is the mission of your organization right? Who do you want to reach? What message do you wish to get over? Who are your potential allies? How can your partners support you? Who are your competitors? At the same time one should not forget that **culture is not a business as any other - it has social and civic dimension**. Last but not least, it is important to choose the right people who are leading the change: one person who has competency for strategic planning should be present; everybody who is responsible for implementation should be involved in the process as well as the organisation's board.

B. Being clear about the mission and the values

Sue Hoyle, Director of Clore Leadership Programme, was of the opinion that **the values in the heart of organization should be incorporated in every action of the leader**. Being a leader is not about status; it is about relationships and approach. Leaders are change makers - they need an appetite to create. They need to be audience-centric and attentional to the needs of others.

She underlined that **audience-centric approach is about consistency, constancy, excellence, adaptability, courage to try new things, and trust with communities**. The mission of the organization has to be clear - it has to identify what it does best. Misconceptions about the mission should be redressed through communication. The leader should be resilient, alert, with the capacity to make difficult decisions and to listen to their own instincts; he or she should not be fearful of the unknown and must have a strong personality. Furthermore, the leader has to be entrepreneurial, good with money and capable of fundraising. **The leader has to advocate for culture in general, not just for his or her organization**. Last but not least, leaders have to be brilliant communicators and negotiators; they need to know about the politics with big and small p. At the end she emphasised that **successful organizations have to take responsibility for their communities.**

C. Fighting against exclusion

Andrew Ormston, founder and Director of Drew Wylie Ltd, highlighted the fact that what we are fighting against today is a social and economic situation which is excluding many people. **In search of new solutions, an audience-centric organization should start with the idea that culture is connected to the whole of society**. He gave some examples, which illustrated how encouraging first contacts between artists and community could bring lasting collaborations. Additionally, **cultural organizations have to take into account digital shift**. Especially with young people, digital inclusion is extremely important. Therefore cultural programmes should aim to enable children and young people to achieve through the arts and creativity.

D. Being part of a larger agenda

Monica Urian de Sousa, Programme Manager at the European Commission – Directorate General Education and Culture – responsible for the 'audience development' priority within the Creative Europe Programme – Culture, welcomed the initiative of Theatron project. Before the European Commission set up the new Creative Europe programme, Theatron had focused on the relevant cultural challenges of today: how to reinvent theatres' approach to audiences in the time of digital shift and other important societal changes that we are facing. She was of the opinion that it is all about people. People are hungry for social engagement. **Accessible and inclusive culture are political priorities of diverse European Commission programmes** like Creative Europe, Erasmus +, and others. However, **cultural priorities are part of a larger agenda that focuses on economical growth, jobs and youth unemployment**. In the future, the European Commission plans to make an expert group about audience development to further support this issue. The European Commission knows a lot about big cultural players but less about the small ones. Therefore the networking initiative of Theatron is even more precious. At the end Monica Urian de Sousa stipulated that **it is extremely important to take the conversation on audiences and culture shift out of the room** and share it with as many people as possible.

CREATING ROADMAPS FOR CHANGE

The Sunday panel served as a wrap up of previous presentations and as a warm up to the workshops on several topics that were approached during the conference.

Sue Hoyle explained that in the process of change it is of key importance to **talk to all kinds of people that are involved in culture**. Monica Urian de Sousa proposed that there should be **exchange programmes between the countries that have important experience** in the field of audience's programmes and those that lack such experience. Andrew Ormston added that we should **follow the example of universities**. They are more involved with their audiences since they have more commitment to the application of their work - at the end of the educational process the students have to get jobs. Lars Seeberg agreed that we should

sciences to create short films aimed at attracting the wider public to deSingel's programming which appear on the organisation's Web site.

Ebbing and flowing audiences

The efforts of deSingel to reach new audiences are made complicated

make bridges between cultural and educational systems. He explained that correlations in the European Commission programmes could mean potential revolution in both sectors. Monica Urian de Sousa found that this kind of bridging would need **more lobbying by cultural sector**. On the question from the audience on how the cultural sector can follow the political objectives for achievement of which it has no tools - such as economical or employment growth, she replied that there is no "or-or" option in current situation. **Cultural sector has to adapt to a wider agenda.**

After the panel, the participants of the conference split into four groups where they exchanged their experiences and ideas on the issues approached during the conference.

---

[1] Dagan Klaić, *Resetting the Stage: Public Theatre Between the Market and Democracy*, first published in the UK in 2012 by Intellect Ltd, Bristol, UK,

PART II

How to Do A Culture.Shift

Benita Lipps, Editor

How To Do A Culture.Shift

Overview of Part II

According to the Wallace Foundation's seminal publication 'Building Arts Organizations that Build Audiences'[1] there are three key factors that must exist in order for a creative house to successfully transform itself into an audience-centric organisation or – in the words of this book – to 'do a Culture.Shift':

- **incentives** – factors that provide a motivation to change,
- **capacity** – the skills to carry it out, and
- **opportunity** – the chance and ability to do things differently.

This book starts by looking at **incentives**: outlining why audience development is becoming increasingly important: Changing demographics, new technology, economic recession, political pressures and – most importantly – new demands by audiences themselves. The desire to "Reset the Stage"[11] artistically provides an important internal motivation. The book will finish with case studies of houses that took the **opportunity** and started doing things differently – hopefully inspiring others to follow suit.

This section will look at the second condition necessary for change: **capacity**. Four experts share their insights on what's needed to instigate and successfully manage a 'Culture.Shift' in performing arts organisations. Each of these contributions highlights a different requirement, a different skill-set that should be developed in organisations that want to become audience-centric.

I) Mindset

The capacity to understand, embrace and internalise the philosophy of an audience-centric organisation (rather than just paying lip service to the latest 'funding buzzword').

II) Evidence

The capacity to identify relevant audience groups and communities – and to understand their needs, interests and desires. This allows an organisation to avoid guesswork and projection and work towards solutions to actual challenges.

III) Strategy

The capacity to align the planning and operations of the entire organisation with the audience-centric mission and follow long-term plans for growing and developing audiences.

IV) Leadership

The capacity to inspire, lead and successfully implement the development of the organisation into an audience-centric one.

These skill-sets are interdependent and connected; indeed it would be hard to develop one without having first mastered the preceding one: There is no point in pursuing a 'Culture.Shift' if one doesn't believe in its value. Similarly, even the most eloquent strategy cannot achieve positive change if it doesn't address real, evidence-based needs and desires. Lastly, a leader without a vision and strategy is unlikely to find the path into a better future.

I) AUDIENCE-CENTRIC MINDSET: AUDIENCE – PEOPLE – PLACE

The Audience Engagement Program of Australia Council for the Arts invites its creative organisations to embark on a big 'shift in thinking' when proclaiming that the "true value of any art is defined by its audience."[III] Whether one agrees with this statement or not, it is a fact that strategic audience development requires a whole new way of thinking. It needs a mind-set that considers (future) audiences as an integral part of the institution, respects their needs and interests, involves their ideas in planning new programmes and makes them a part of the institution.[IV]

In the first article of this section, Andrew Ormston argues that there may still be a bit of 'shifting' to do: He points out that –despite a genuine desire by creative leaders to maximise access to their work – most have not yet embedded audience engagement into their daily practice. He shows that audience engagement cannot happen through one-way consumption of predefined content. It requires organisations to actively connect with people and places, and work towards transformative encounters between performing arts organisations and their communities. The article argues that creative leaders need to reinvigorate their organisation's commitment to social inclusion – not just by developing new models and schemes, but by ensuring a 'whole organisational' response.

II) EVIDENCE: EVIDENCE-BASED AUDIENCE DEVELOPMENT

A second step of the 'Culture.Shift' is getting to know the people you are trying to engage. Arts organisations that want to build their audiences need to get to know their audiences. Once an organisation understands the patterns of audience interests, desires and behaviour, it can identify opportunities for development – both in terms of artistic production and operational viability.

There may still be artistic directors that are rather sceptical when it comes to giving market research a voice when it comes to the development of the house, fearing that giving power to 'marketeers' may infringe on their artistic autonomy and vision. However, letting audience information inform your strategy is not the same as changing an artistic mission. According to Patti Isaacson, deputy director of Seattle's Experience Music Project, "A sustained use of data can help you intentionally plan as opposed to feeling that you have to be reactive or make decisions that you don't want to do."[V]

This point is discussed more thoroughly by Achim Müller in this second article. He shows that any audience development strategy needs to be grounded in empirical knowledge about one's audience and the nature of their relationship with the organisation. The article outlines six principles that any cultural organisation should bear in mind when designing audience research.

III) STRATEGY: WHY CHANGE?

Unfortunately, people don't spontaneously transform from non-attendees into dedicated audience members after a single visit, no matter how good and relevant the performance. One-off promotions and short-term outreach activities are therefore unlikely to lead to sustainable results in audience development. Studies show us that what is required, is persistence – and a long-term plan: "all evidence about sustained arts engagement suggests that it springs from a comfort level and special relation-

ship developed over multiple experiences." [VI]

How can arts organisations embed audience development into their strategy and operations, so newcomers become repeat attendees? This is the question Graham Devlin addresses in this third article.

He explains why organisations that wish to be more audience-centric need to change their strategy. The article gives some pointers as to how such a change can be achieved and encourages houses to analyse their circumstances and their offer before investing in change. Only when an organisation knows where they are, can they plan where to go. The article then describes how to create internal ownership for the new direction, ensuring that the entire house is supporting the development. Finally, it provides some hands-on tips for implementing the new strategy.

IV) LEADERSHIP: CREATIVITY AND COMMUNITY

Changing the strategic outlook of an organisation requires time and effort from all those involved. Consequently, the fourth and final step of the 'Culture.Shift' is concerned with people: people with a vision and willing to make a change.

Building audiences starts with the vision and will of the leadership of an organisation. As Sue Hoyle explains in her article, this creative leadership is not necessarily determined by status, position or job title: A creative leader can be any member of organisation, as long as she or he choses "to make a difference to – and through – culture."

In fact, creative leadership is a task for the entire organisation: from front-of-house staff to board members. This isn't limited to the operations and marketing people, but specifically includes the artistic leaders of the house. "Artistic directors can help us ask new questions," confirms Tom Kaiden, president of the Greater Philadelphia Cultural Alliance.[VII] "There may be questions that management hadn't thought of that help give patrons more of a voice."

In her article, Sue Hoyle outlines five principles of audience-centric leadership that apply across functions and departments: constancy, excellence & relevance, curiosity, courage and trust. Based on the experiences gained though the Clore Leadership programme, she provides an overview of critical qualities and skills we should be developing as creative leaders.

REFERENCES

[I] The Wallace Foundation (2012): Building Arts Organizations that Build Audiences

[II] Dragan Klaic (2012): Resetting the Stage

[III] http://australiacouncil.gov.au/arts-in-daily-life/artist-stories/connecting-with-your-audience/

[IV] Birgit Mandel (2013): Audience Development

[V] The Wallace Foundation (2012) Building Arts Organizations That Build Audiences p.7

[VI] Birgit Mandel (2013) Audience Development, p.10

[VII] The Wallace Foundation (2012) Building Arts Organizations That Build Audiences p.9

Andrew Ormston, Drew Wylie Projects

Audience – People – Place

Cultural production is, on the whole, a supplier led process. Creating work is cherished as practice that is exempt from the full discipline of the demand side. Cultural policy and related interventions are, as a consequence, about closing the loop of artist, audience, people and place. However, policy is failing to keep up with the scale and pace of economic, social and cultural change. Many people no longer see the established main-stream arts as a significant part of their lives. Can we keep focus on the creative process, or do we go where the market takes us?

The Culture Shift meeting took place in Antwerp, overwhelming me with memories of my last visit, aged 16, as apprentice on the SS Border Castle. This was a formative time and included my first experience of the programming ethos I later came to know as 'the balanced' approach to arts programming. A quasi-commercial approach where the tribute music act or touring musical makes the box office income that allows you to promote the contemporary dance or music that doesn't. In Antwerp, in 1972, this meant taking on the three 16mm films that would be our on-board entertainment for a run to Port Salem. I adopted a philosophy that I would later apply in a range of concert halls, theatres and arts centres. One for the Deck Officers, one for the Engineers and one for me. In this case, 1972, I think it was Cabaret, The Poseidon Adventure, and Solaris. In my 1992 role it may

have been The Madness of George III, Buddy, and Rosas. The result was the same - happy deck officers, engineers and culture vultures.

There are venues in the UK that are less tied to balanced programme economics. The major art houses are subsidised to focus on the art. London's West End is a commercial powerhouse with the figures to match: almost 15m. attendances and over £585m. of box office income in 2013. However, across the length and width of the UK, programme balancing is the name of the programming game. Many of these theatres and concert halls could almost be called relics of the pre-cinema age. They were taken on by local authorities due to market failure, a process that began with cinema and ended with television. This led to hybridisation of commercial and subsidised programming, an approach which also informs the artistic and business plans of the newer phase of arts centre developments. Migration of civic venues to independent 'not for profit' Trusts was a logical next step in allowing for arts subsidies and for more enterprising trading.

The performing arts and theatre in particular, is a mixed economy of intertwined commercial, public and charitable interests and models. The positive outcomes of this approach are many and various, and can be seen in every Oscar ceremony or major city theatre quarter. The story since the banking crash is familiar to everyone, as its implications work through producers, promoters and audiences. Market economics is the absolutely dominant recipe in the UK. Again there have been many positive results, with commercial transfers from the subsidised theatre sector proving to be some of the most successful shows on both Broadway and the West End. But there has been a cost. Whereas access to culture may be considered a basic human right in most of Europe, in the UK, value of access to culture is defined as wealth creating. As I write this English National Opera have been taken in hand ('special measures') by Arts Council England [1] for a failure to adopt a realistic business model, one which will include a partnership with West End musical producers. Commercial success and failure are different sides of the same coin. In this example it is the artistic leadership of the organisation that is under pressure, but the more pervasive result throughout the cultural sector has been the rise of exclusivity.

Last year's Telegraph interview with Kevin Spacey raised alarm bells as he worried about theatre becoming an exclusive club and ticket prices driving young people away, with the average West End theatre ticket now about €68. However, business remains brisk and the same article quoted a €712m. West End theatre box office in 2011, and talked about the variety of cheap seats made available through sponsors at the Old Vic and the National. More recently the shadow culture minister, Chris Bryant, raised eyebrows with his concerns over the privileged backgrounds of today's performers and a closing off of meritocratic progression routes. His call for a fairer arts funding system is to address concerns of a hollowing out of the arts, with whole sections of society no longer either explored by, or engaged with the sector [2].

As I was penning this paper a twitter ex-change between two leading cultural researchers popped up: "Cultural value & inequality: for non-white, non-middle class people, institutionalised culture just does not seem relevant to their lives" @DrDaveOBrien; "the @UoWcommission will raise a similar concern...." @elebelfiore.

Institutionalised culture has never seemed very relevant to my life either, so I wondered what we mean by the term. If it means culture that needs a major mechanism to deliver it then that applies to everything from cinema, to a music festival, to a museum. If it means culture that needs longevity beyond the limits of an individual's lifespan, then that applies to rock and roll, opera, sculpture, and fashion. If it means institutions that promote exclusivity through habit, price or avarice then that can apply to any form of culture, from the private view, to the after-show. What I think it actually refers to are the institutions that prepare us to engage with culture, and predominantly family and school. In some ways a return to Raymond Williams and his influential view of culture as a whole way of life. The question becomes what is the cultural composition of that way of life. We need to understand this to be able to make sure the loop of audience, people and place works. If art is a transformative encounter then people only become audiences at that moment, and most audience experiences need both artist and person to bring something to the experience.

For someone like me an equality of access to the arts is a fundamental concept. One that is akin to the philosopher John Rawls's idea of a range property [3]. Rawls rooted his work in two principles of which the first 'guarantees the right of each person to have the most extensive basic liberty compatible with the liberty of others', and he attempts to deal with an understanding of equality where clear differences can apply. For example one theatre goer may be attending a mid-scale performance of Othello in a local arts centre while another may be seeing the same play performed by the RSC on the main stage in Stratford. Both audience members share a range value of a live performance of Othello and are therefore equal in those terms. We know that not everyone can see a RSC performance at Stratford. However, we could have an expectation that everyone could have the option of attending a live theatre performance. The question is what are the 'property ranges' that we should be working to achieve. For example, for some, an event cinema or online streaming of Othello should be in the same property range as the live performance. Whereas others, including myself, would argue that the power of the live encounter with theatre disqualifies it.

We have worked so hard to engage people with the performing arts. Chris Bryant used the example of the London's National Theatre opening on to the river, and not to the population of South London that sits behind it. I was reminded of one of Jude Kelly's first steps when appointed to the adjacent South Bank Centre. She simply reoriented the centre so a public face was presented to local residents. The centre remains an oasis where free local culture rubs shoulders with the stars of the classical arts.

However, the current situation of the cultural sector is not just ripe for reflection, it is also a cause of real anger and hurt as people see their work denied to increasing numbers of people, and a kind of cultural poverty take hold. Can we understand how this is happening with the help of a sociologist like Saskia Sassen? Sassen explores how soaring income inequality has led to the expelling of increasing numbers of "people, enterprises and places from the core social and economic orders of our time" [4]. She talks of 'predatory formations', a mix of elites and systemic capacities that produce acute concentrations of wealth. So on the one hand, we have a 60% growth in wealth of the wealthiest 1% over the last 20 years, but on the other, what makes this possible is a complex system of actors and government enablement. The result is an 'impenetrable haze' where it is difficult to see what is happening. If we make the assumption that we are also witnessing some expelling from our core cultural order, then are we able to see through the haze to what is happening? Sassen thinks that you can't see the robber barons any more, and this might be the case in the global creative industries but we have more transparency in our more intimate arts and culture economy. After all Ambassadors Group or Bozars are not major hedge funds. However, we have to be attentive as the tools of expulsion still apply. A theatre ticket becomes a hopelessly unaffordable luxury. A performance is something that 'isn't for the likes of me'. The subject and treatment of material is not appli-

cable to my income or ethnic group. I recently evaluated a major research project, the AHRC funded 'The Staging of the Scottish Renaissance Court' [5], that involved staging a famous 16th Century play, Sir David Lyndsay's 'Satire of the Three Estates'. So many of the participants and audience were struck by the simple fact that a central character, the pauper or poor man, was the wise and ethical heart of the piece. The actors made the obvious comparison with Shakespeare where wisdom and resolution usually comes with a crown. The re-staging of the play was considered to be dramatic time travel by actors who witnessed how the performative process brought the Scots language and the politics of the piece to life for a diverse audience.

So not only do we have to identify the 'range properties' we want people to have, but we need to actively fight against the socio-economic forces that work against these basic cultural equalities. It may be that Sassen's 'expulsions' applies more to the arts case for investment - the form, content, and distribution of work - than expelling people from arts and culture. Most of the cultural sector is populated with professionals that want to maximise access and are genuinely concerned about the thinning of the audience profile. The fact is, however, that we have consistently failed to embed audience engagement and arts development in arts practice. It remains a luxury and something that can be dispensed with when times are hard. I recently attended a Scottish Parliament Working Group on Culture [6] where the Chair asked the assembled arts and culture professionals whether supporting culture should be a mandatory Governmental obligation. This was met with confused silence only a decade or so after sustained campaigns to do just that. There must be an argument for access to cultural infrastructure wherever you live.

There are examples of work that sustains. The Cultural Affairs Committee of the Council of Europe is currently examining 'cultural and creative crossovers' as it grapples with culture's contribution to the economy and social inclusion. This prompted me to re-appraise two projects that I worked with over a decade ago. Both survive, and both require major cultural organisations to behave in different ways to their traditional core purpose. Arts and culture infrastructure and capacity tends to be concentrated in city centres, as evidenced by the influential 'Rebalancing Our Cultural Capital' report in 2013 [7]. There is a place for schemes that connect up the cultural organisations of city centres with the localities where most people live. The following examples demonstrate two sides of the same approach. The Arts Champions Scheme connects each of the 12 major arts organisations in Birmingham with one of the 10 Districts that comprise the city. Gallery 37 connects talented but marginalised people, and particularly young people, from the wider city with Birmingham's cultural heart through a short term intensive apprenticeship programme situated and showcased in the city centre [8].

The Arts Champions Scheme was launched in 2004 to coincide with the 'localisation' of some of the Birmingham's services into new districts, each with a population of around 100,000. The city is home to 12 major arts organisations, ranging from Birmingham Royal Ballet, to the IKON Gallery, to The Rep theatre. The Champions scheme simply obligated each organisation to partner with a new district to identify and deliver activity that would make a difference. The Champions shortlisted districts they would like to work in, and were supported by the City Council in making initial contacts and relationships at local level. There was no prescription and activity could range from establishing youth theatres or choirs, to a dance leadership scheme to engaging hard to reach groups, to the development of craft skills. The scheme helped form Birmingham's 'Culture on Your Doorstep' strategy and was formally adopted as a Local Arts Protocol in 2009 and now has a common evaluation framework. There are four guiding principles:

1. improve cultural infrastructure to ensure that residents have access to high quality cultural opportunities in their neighbourhoods

2. invent new ways of connecting city-centre based resources to local neighbourhoods, which make our cultural assets more accessible
3. develop ways to communicate the range of cultural opportunities in local neighbour-hoods
4. increase participation by local residents in targeted neighbour-hoods

The Champions reside in their District for a period of three years before starting a relationship with another district. The organisations are encouraged to both maintain contact with their previous district, and to facilitate the incoming Champion. Their role has been formalised as:

- advocate for the arts sector in neighbour-hoods giving advice and support
- provide a catalyst for locally developed arts programmes
- provide activities in local neighbourhoods and linking local communities to city centre provision.

Participation in the scheme is included within each Champions overall funding agreement with the City Council and a small additional sum of £4,000 per District is available to help lever funds from other places. Local arts audiences and levels of arts participation have increased significantly during the life of the scheme (doubling between 2011 and 2013). A case study of the scheme was taken up by

Eurocities and similar initiatives in Helsinki and Lyon have been informed and partly inspired by the Arts Champions scheme.

The Arts Champions scheme demonstrates an effective and simple model that connects audience, people and place. The next scheme is more complex in that it sets out to transform the prospects of people who are currently marginalised from the cultural sector. Nevertheless, the scheme depends on recruiting talented people, locating them in an intensively creative environment, and linking them with arts organisations and professionals.

Gallery 37 was initiated in Birmingham by the City Council's Arts and Events team in 1998. It developed from a model of creative arts training, set in a "canvas village", that was pioneered in Birmingham's sister city Chicago. The Birmingham version, delivered in a purpose built pagoda tented structure in Birmingham city centre, quickly established an identity, style and reputation of its own, providing a format appropriate to the creative training and support for young people in a major culturally diverse city. The aim was to provide a quality work experience for young people and to: raise aspirations of socially excluded people through the arts; actively promote arts and arts organisations in the city; be pro-active in partnership work and artistic collaborations; provide professional training for community artists.

Each year a team of artists, working in association with Birmingham's arts organisations used a series of hands on projects as a vehicle for an intensive, high quality training experience. By 2002 nearly two hundred young people each year were passing through the Gallery 37 annual programme. Of these over 90% were achieving positive outcomes in terms of employment or further full-time training.

Applicants were actively recruited from hard to reach groups and submitted work or auditioned to secure entry to the scheme. The initial focus was on marginalised young people, but subsequent years have also targeted elderly people and people with learning disabilities. The city centre base was a key aspect of the scheme, both introducing young people to the cultural heart of Birmingham, and their work to the wide range of people working and visiting the centre. It also meant that young people were given 'breathing space' from pressures that they may be experiencing in their local situation. In addition to training for young people Gallery 37 also provided a fertile training ground for artists and practitioners wishing to develop workshop and training skills. Increasingly young participants/apprentices returned to Gallery 37 themselves, as trainee artists, completing a cycle of excellence which

generated extraordinary opportunities for young people to embark on a practical career in the arts.

While the scheme was very successful and widely admired the ratio of expenditure in relation to numbers of participants was higher than the norm. The cost of a Gallery 37 "apprenticeship" was around €2,840 per person. This meant that securing investment to operate the scheme has always been a challenge and the project is not taking place in 2015. However, plans are being developed to run G37 in 2016 as a "foundation apprenticeship" linked to a wider skills agenda. Gallery 37 has collaborated with a range of organisations to develop the model elsewhere in the UK. For example Impact Arts in Scotland is operating G37 projects in Ayrshire and in Edinburgh in 2015. The critical success factor for this project was the quality of the apprenticeship experience, and the involvement of the city's major arts organisations and practitioners was a key element to securing high standards.

There is, of course, a wide range of inspiring work going on to connect audience, people and place. For example I am currently working as a critical friend for the Creative People and Places programme in Corby [9]. This is an ambitious initiative that where local communities in 21 locations across England least well served by arts provision are devising arts programmes that respond to their priorities. The aggregated project aims to make a major contribution to how arts activity is planned, resourced and delivered. The Scottish referendum experience was also inspiring as cultural organisations were in the heart of the campaigning and debate. 'The Great Yes, No, Don't Know 5 minute theatre show' curated by the National Theatre of Scotland was a great example of how digital tools can connect culture across a wide spectrum of interests, with contributions across a 24 hour period from the widest imaginable cohort of artists, schools and communities [10].

There is, however, a growing problem. The ENO situation was described by the company's director in residence, Peter Sellars, as a "Chernobyl meltdown", a cultural meltdown that is affecting the performing arts sector as a whole. Chris Bryant talks of a "cultural drought" outside of London. Perhaps we have just forgotten how to work our cultural assets? The dominant creative narrative is currently one of entrepreneurship. While this is a healthy drive to innovation, it foregrounds the monetising tip of the cultural iceberg. We can lose focus on both the social and collaborative aspects of creative production and the social environment in which it operates.

CONCLUSIONS

The inescapable truth is that we need to keep supporting both the supply and demand sides of culture. If we only invest in production then it will become more and more exclusive. If we only focus on demand then we lose our creative capacity. We need to reinvigorate our cultural organisation's commitment to social inclusion. There may be a need for new models, but there is also a need for a 'whole organisational' response from arts institutions, from Board member to technical staff.

There is an unshakeable founding notion for many of us. We believe that art changes lives. Much of that art comes to us from 'institutions' that constantly reinvent the traditions of classical culture, from the orchestral symphony to Kathak dance. We need to keep faith with this belief in the transformative power of the artistic encounter. We need to keep working to make sure everyone experiences it.

REFERENCES AND FURTHER READING

[I] Mark Brown. **The Guardian**. [Website] Available: http://www.theguardian.com/culture/2015/feb/12/english-national-opera-told-to-put-its-house-in-order

[II] Rowena Mason. **The Guardian**. [Website] Available: http://www.theguardian.com/politics/2015/jan/16/arts-diversity-chris-bryant-eddie-redmayne

[III] John Rawls, A Theory of Justice, The Belknap Press of Harvard University Press, 1971

[IV] Saskia Sassen, Expulsions - Brutality and Complexity in the Global Economy, The Belknap Press of Harvard University Press, 2014

[V] http://www.stagingthescottishcourt.org

[VI] http://www.scottish.parliament.uk/msps/68054.aspx

[VII] http://www.gpsculture.co.uk/rocc.php

[VIII] Information provided by Birmingham City Council

[IX] http://creativepeopleplaces.org.uk

[X] http://www.nationaltheatrescotland.com/content/default.asp?page=home_TheGreatYesNoDontKnowFiveMinuteTheatreShow

Achim Müller, Zentrums für Audience Development am Institut für Kultur- und Medienmanagement der Freien Universität Berlin

Evidence-Based Audience Development

The need for audience development in culture, the Arts and theatres in specific has been widely discussed. European societies are changing and are subject to severe strains because of economic imbalances and migration both within and from outside of Europe. In the field of leisure activities the societal role of the Arts is questioned due to the obvious convergence between entertainment and the Arts. In the light of these developments it has become critical for the Arts and for theatre to establish and intensify relationships with existing and new audiences. Only by doing so they will be a relevant participant of society and maintain the legitimacy for their existence, be it through public, private or corporate funding.

RESEARCH QUESTIONS IN AN INTEGRATED SYSTEM OF AUDIENCE DEVELOPMENT

Leadership of an arts organisation that embraces audience development in order to meet the challenges of the current reality has to be grounded in empirical knowledge about their audience, the public and the nature of their relationship to the organisation. Starting from an operational definition of audience development as a task of systemic management, research in the context of audience development has to be ready to address informational needs. Basic principles need to be outlined for the setup of research that provides valid evidence for these needs; principles illustrated by references to solutions initiated by the EU-funded theatre network Theatron.

To be comprehensive, research questions within audience development have to be derived from a broad definition of the topic. To have a sustainable effect on arts organisations, audience development should be regarded as a comprehensive and integrative organisational practise that focuses all activities of an arts organisation on the audience and more generally on the public as a potential or general audience.

The implementation of audience development within this integrative definition includes all areas of an arts organisation. For systemic consistency, these areas can be structured into normative, strategic and operational. The following table (next page) shows examples of the type of research questions leaders will need empirical evidence for in their pursuit of audience development.

Management level and exemplary tasks	Exemplary question for empirical research
Normative management - Vision, mission, claims, values	- What values and overall objectives are the public and the audience searching to realise through their attendance or participation in activities in culture and arts?
Strategic management - Target audiences, identity & image, positioning & brand building, core strategies, objectives	- Which parts of the society are included in our audience, which are not? - What are their habits and preferences toward culture and leisure activities? How can they be formed? - How is our identity perceived (image)? - Which strategies do other theatres implement? With which success?
Operational management - Repertory/program, artists, staging/directing, prices, ticketing, communications, services, building, atmosphere, co-operations	- How are different parts of our artistic or other activities perceived and valued? - Did a specific type of performance or other activity attract the audience it was meant for? - What specific channels should be used to communicate with a specific target group?

The examples show that on each level of audience development empirical evidence is critical in the realisation of the overall objective: to establish lasting bonds with existing and new audiences.

PRINCIPLES FOR EMPIRICAL RESEARCH

Each of the following principles answers to specific challenges encountered when performing empirical research in audience development. Each principle will be illustrated by an example from the Theatron network.

Define what you really have to know.

In the perception of many arts organisations there are only a handful of standard formats of audience research. Yet the informational needs in each case may differ because of a large number of factors: the composition of the audience, the aspect of a performance to be evaluated, the management level on which a decision is needed, the extent of prior knowledge. Thus for each research case, the research subjects have to be carefully developed from the aims and challenges of the organisation.

In Theatron each research case begins with a preparatory meeting between the organisation and the Institute for Arts and Media Management (IKM) of Freie Universität Berlin where the specific research subjects are identified and combined with subjects familiar from other projects.

Combine Quantitative and Qualitative Methods.

The relationship between a visitor or potential visitor and an arts organisation is always the result of a complex interaction between the offers and the identity of the organisation and the habits, preferences and motivations of the visitor. Frequently these patterns are shaped by specific regional conditions.

The complex interaction between these factors very often can only be understood through qualitative methods like in-depth interviews or focus groups. Yet these qualitative methods lack statistical representativity that allows researchers to judge the relevance of a relationship in the overall audience. Therefore, for each research case, a suitable combination of quantitative instruments for statistically representative figures and qualitative instruments for complex, content-based and in-depth-understanding should be chosen.

In the research in Theatron, qualitative and quantitative research is often set up in consecutive order. A quantitative audience survey may be followed by focus groups with target groups that were discovered to be underrepresented in the audience.

Assure data coherence.

Especially when working with several research methods as proposed above the danger arises that the results do not combine into an integrated answer to research questions, instead answering to different aspects each. To avoid this inefficiency, all questionnaires and guidelines should be derived from the same core of research subjects.

Theatron assesses a modular set of questions to be used as a basis for quantitative surveys and a modular guideline to be used in quantitative interviews. These were designed from a common set of research subjects. By using the same basic question data coherence and comparability is ensured.

Control the Quality of Sampling.

Very often the budget of arts organisations does not allow outsourcing of the data collection to a professional service provider. Moreover in theatres it is often more adequate to distribute questionnaires through front-of-house staff as these have an already established relationship to the audience that enhances participation. The same is true for the recruiting of interview partners or participants for group discussions.

Yet the application of randomized distribution in audience surveys and the diversity of participants for interviews are critical for the validity of data. Flaws at this stage might mean that the results do not reflect the reality encountered in the theatre without being noticed. As a consequence, the project responsible should implement simple, reliable and controllable methods for random sampling and thoroughly recruit, train and control the sampling personal. In qualitative research, the diversity of participants has to be ensured.

Because of the high relevance of this topic, in Theatron experts train any member of the staff that participates in the distribution of questionnaires on site and monitors the start of data collection. Also the criteria for the choice of participants in qualitative research are set up by this project responsible.

Integrate Analytical and Artistic Expertise in the Analysis.

The relationship between an arts organisation and its existing or potential audience not only relies on regional characteristics as mentioned above. It is formed in the highly complex interaction between artists, content, technical abilities, aesthetics, atmosphere and reputation on the side of a theatre and preferences, habits, prior experience, social status, own artistic activities (among others) on the side of the (potential) visitor. The complexity is augmented as the social surrounding of the visitor together with media and other influences also interfere.

To analyse and interpret this complex pattern, it is of great value if the researcher combines both analytical expertise to apply the methods correctly and profound practical experience in the cultural field. If this is provided, the analysis can already integrate the artistic perspective into the presentation of results to the leader of the arts organisation.

Within Theatron, the research partner IKM allocated two experts to the project that had both scientific training and practical experience in leading positions in arts organisations.

Facilitate the Result Implementation.

A lot of empirical research in the Arts has failed to have substantial effect. Very often this is due to the fact that the persons that have to implement the conclusions and recommendations into practice are only included in the research process when the final results are presented.

The impact of research can be largely augmented when persons from the arts organisation that work with the results at a later date are included in the process as early as possible.

When research is set up in Theatron, each of the participating partners is encouraged to invite persons from relevant departments to already participate in the preparatory meeting where the research subjects are set up. Also the results are presented before rendering the final version of the report. Thereby questions and additional in-depth analysis answering the specific interest of the organisation are included in a working document in the literal sense.

CONCLUSIONS

Audience development has to be considered as a comprehensive and integrated organisation practice that engulfs all levels of management. A need for empirical evidence arises on each of the management levels. From this observation a set of principles has been proposed that together ensures that research performed along these guidelines provides valid and applicable evidence.

At best this understanding of research leads to close collaborations between research and leaderships in cycles of gathering evidence and the practice of audience development. It can also produce a common understanding of the situation and eventually lead to better informed and dynamically improved decisions in a shifting environment.

Graham Devlin, Independent Cultural Strategist

Why Change?

WHY DO ORGANISATIONS WHO WISH TO BE MORE AUDIENCE-CENTRIC WANT OR NEED TO CHANGE?

WHY CHANGE AT ALL?

There are different drivers behind the decision for organisations to change to become more audience-centric which can be broadly categorised as voluntary and involuntary - or alternatively, strategic or desperate.

Change can be forced upon organisations by the profound pressures emerging from the political and financial landscape, specifically declining income arising from both local and national government cutbacks. Cultural organisations of all kinds need to review every aspect of their operation to ensure maximum return on both public and private investment.

Societal shifts can also inspire change. Ageing populations, increasing cultural diversity, massive diversification of leisure options and platforms, the rise of digital media and social networking, climate change and the nature of public space are just some of the drivers which influence a transformation in an organisation's approach to audience patterns which are uncertain, especially in terms of box-office spend.

Particular organisation-specific issues can also have a change-inducing effect, such as losing audiences or funding; the necessity of a new building, a change of leadership, and the new opportunities

Organisations also have to adapt in line with the increased emphasis on collaborations and entrepreneurialism, and the blurring of the distinction between creation and consumption with new ways of working – including exploiting the potential of the Internet. Traditional models of production are becoming increasingly challenged as new technology and platforms allow young people to create their art at home on laptops.

Particular organisation-specific issues also matter - losing audiences or funding; a new building, change of leadership, new opportunities. In each case, it's essential to analyse the real reason for the need to change and whether the proposed solution is the right one (especially if it has big cost implications like building works). Sometimes the analysis is faulty and an organisation tries to answer the wrong question.

These factors can easily seem overwhelming. We must think our way strategically through them for three reasons. Firstly, cultural organisations which become fixated on current, immediate economic events run the risk of overlooking core issues; this leads to the organisation not seeing beyond the uncertainty to longer term strategies. Secondly, challenging as the current situation may be, it won't reverse some fundamental trends - such as the ageing of consumers in Europe and North America, the continuing economic development of Brazil, Russia India, and China, or the technological developments of the creative industries. Finally, given the scale of the changes of the last few years, cultural organizations already have a body of experience of navigating through choppy waters. They are better prepared now to anticipate and work towards new strategies that are change-responsive.

To do that, we have to be prepared to transform; we need to change our working habits, our priorities, perhaps even the work that we do and the way that we do it. And any such strategy for transformation has to serve both the art and audiences. It should be art-centred and audience-focused. It mustn't be a constraint on artistic creativity, a document on a shelf or a stick to beat someone with. Rather, it must balance artistic imper-atives and organizational efficiencies. It should be a directional tool; dynamic and living.

Changing the Royal Court

The Royal Court in London is the UK's foremost new writing theatre and possibly the leading English-language new writing company in the world. But new writing is tricky – certainly in the UK. It's an 'unknown' and often 'difficult'. It demands a huge amount of trust from the audience – and from other stakeholders like corporate sponsors. Ten years ago, this was presenting challenges to the Royal Court – both in terms of audiences and income. It was seen as 'worthy' but hard work. The company put the principle of attracting new audiences at the heart of their thinking. They produced a string of critically acclaimed shows – some of which were controversial. But new audiences came in: both from the traditional theatre-going public who might have thought the Court wasn't 'for them' and also – in some aspects of the programme - from under-privileged areas. This was commercial success without betraying the mission or the quality.

As a result, audience trust has built. In the last four seasons the Court's two theatres averaged over 95% occupancy overall. And box office income has risen by 25%. It's also secured a number of West End and Broadway transfers and many major awards. This was done by broadening the range of work on the main stage to make it more entertaining whilst maintaining challenge and innovation; exploring different media (e.g. micro-plays commissioned in partnership with The Guardian newspaper and made available on both partners' websites); creating Theatre Local – a pop up theatre that goes into under-privileged London communities with new work, and re-focusing its international writers' development programme to connect those writers with relevant communities in London.

As a consequence of all these initiatives, the Court's 'Friends' scheme has increased 10-fold, its Arts Council grant has held up fairly well through a period of severe cuts and its commercial sponsorship is transformed with a range of committed partners.

All this is directly a result of the theatre's vision, its commitment to quality, its leadership - which is critically and increasingly important in arts organisations - and its preparedness to transform itself strategically, including through hard choices, streamlining staff to free up money for investment in strategic initiatives such as Theatre Local, play development and enhancing productions.

IDENTIFYING THE NEED FOR CHANGE

Despite the need for change being driven by a variety of circumstances, a few lessons can be drawn which may be useful:

- First, you need a clear analysis of your circumstances and your offer. Do they fit each other?
- Is the Mission still right?
- What audience do you have/want? Who are you trying to reach? Who aren't you reaching? Are you happy with that?
- What is the operating environment – civic, regional, national. Who are your competitors, potential collaborators? Can you take on potential new roles (e.g. as civic anchors, thus becoming essential to you town/city/region)?
- What are your organisational characteristics? What are realistic objectives for your change programme? What might be the implications and risks?
- What are you/ might you be very good at (Strengths and Opportunities)? Focus on those (whilst remaining aware of your weaknesses and vulnerabilities). What is your capacity - and your development needs? Don't set yourself up to fail.
- How strong are your staff/board relationships (because they will be tested)? How clear is your organisational focus? How effective are you?
- How are you viewed? What message does your brand and building send?

- What do you need in order to address all these issues? Do you have/ can you get the right resources (including human) to realise your ambition and reach out to audiences? And be honest: don't avoid difficult questions.
- Who are your potential allies? It's much better to work <u>with</u> than <u>against.</u>
- How can you use the change process to build external relationships (with audiences, funders, partners and stakeholders)? Be inclusive and communicate clearly what you're doing.
- Are there new models that should be considered?

NEW MODELS – EXAMPLES OF LATERAL THINKING

Diversification - Examples

- an organisation that, for many years, ran development ' labs' to enable not-for-profit arts organisations to develop artistic ideas, began to apply the same techniques – and charging - to work with creative industry commercial businesses in order to generate income;
- A theatre, beside which a major building development was taking place, developed its catering business to provide lunches for 300 building workers

- A dance centre developed an adjacent building with accommodation for visiting artists, reducing costs and generating income (and a theatre that did the same whilst also developing a commercial restaurant and bar to service the local area).
- Working with a media partner to achieve better, cheaper communications

Partnerships - Examples

- Three national agencies covering forests, waterways and historic properties working together to develop an integrated public art policy

Mergers - Examples

- Nine small literature/literacy/free expression organisations with little by way of individual resources jointly acquiring and running a building to house them all and develop an integrated year-round programme;
- Two science and industry museums in London and Manchester coming together to share collections, staff etc.

THE OWNERSHIP OF CHANGE

Organisations often have to take 'their people' with them on what is often a difficult journey which may well involve unwelcome choices. If change endangers jobs, staff will be disturbed and fearful. And some will - understandably - remain angry. So it is vital that they understand why change is essential. And recognize that the organisation values them and will do whatever it can to support them if their role is changed or lost. Generosity of spirit is essential to this. An understanding and ownership of the process is critical. So how is that done?

Broad Ownership of the process and the vision is crucial but the process must be clearly led by a planning team with a clear brief and membership criteria. The team should include at least one person who has authority to make strategic decisions – ideally both the chief executive and board chair should be members - and should drive development and implementation of the plan.

The people who will be responsible for implementation should be involved in the planning. Use a cross-functional team (representatives from each part of the organization – ideally at different levels of seniority) to ensure the plan is realistic and collaborative. Continue asking them: "Is this realistic? Is it do-able?"

- Involve everybody in the analysis process through discussions and workshops
- Invite involvement from as many stakeholders (board, staff, audiences/ customers, partners, funders) as is practicable. This keeps the process open and transparent, gives appropriate communities an opportunity to provide feedback and gives you valuable insights
- Consider keeping Board consultation discrete. If you invite your board to attend public sessions, encourage them to hold back their comments and input until they have their own session(s) in order not to over-influence (or alienate) the voices of others.
- Staff member consultations should also be done separately. Your staff knows the organization from the inside so will have a very perceptive analysis. They are likely to be more open (and constructively critical) with ideas on how to improve the organization if they are not on public display

IMPLEMENTING THE PLAN

- Distribute the plan in draft, as appropriate, inviting input.
- Organize it into manageable chunks (smaller action plans) – maybe for each part of the organization or particular initiatives
- Regularly involve people who will be responsible for implementation of the plan
- Cascade the strategic plan's headlines, into practical actions, job descriptions etc.

- Specify roles and responsibilities - who is doing what and by when – and review when necessary. Things will change over time.
- Be diligent about monitoring, evaluating and communicating its progress to ensure it continues to follow the strategic direction
- Be clear that one person has designated responsibility for the plan being enacted in a timely and effective fashion. Build in regular reviews of progress
- The Chief Executive's support of the plan is a major driver to the plan's implementation. Ensure this.
- Take the time it needs - you'll get stuck at points. Allow the time to get unstuck
- Identify the organisational and financial resources required and adapt as necessary:
- Be ambitious, but be real; don't make fantastical assumptions
- Be rigorous both in the process and the analysis.
- Prioritise - Be prepared to make choices.
- Remember that plans are frameworks - guidelines. When circumstances change, so must the plan
- Accept uncertainty (and ambiguity)
- Also remember, the better you plan, the luckier you get

AN EXAMPLE OF CHANGE

The theatre in Derby operated, in an intermittently troubled way – including a period of bankruptcy - from 1975 to 2011 when Arts Council England withdrew funding and a turnaround exercise was begun. On the first day of that process the City Council also withdrew all its funding. A consultancy process identified a number of unique circumstances which offered the theatre a possible future – e.g. it was based in the town centre and owned by a very entrepreneurial University which contained a number of performing arts faculties but lacked practical spaces for workshops and academic development. A plan was developed to re-designate the organisation as a Learning Theatre, involving:

- running a mixture of in-house professional productions and co-productions
- designating a group of associate companies,
- hosting incoming tours
- developing a sophisticated programme of learning and training,
- re-locating many of the academic staff into the building to work closely alongside a re-structured team of professional theatre-makers and managers.

As a result, the theatre has transformed from a traditional producing house to an organisation of and artistic quality, training and mentorship, with a new and inspirational artistic director. It is acknowledged as a national exemplar of excellence in theatre and learning, producing high quality professional theatre, interwoven with learning opportunities at every level for audiences, artists, participants, students and communities. In the last two years, the theatre has:

- Received a raft of excellent reviews,
- Evolved a number of co-production partnerships
- Created a festival showcase for a wide range of small-scale regional/ national companies and provided a developmental support programme for them
- Developed a suite of pre-professional training and higher education courses based in the Theatre, delivered by industry professionals and connected to its professional programme.
- Established Plus One, a unique partnership with Barnardo's charity to enable young people in care to access the arts
- Won the Best Director award in the TMA 2013 UK Awards for its co-production of The Seagull,
- Won the Times Higher Education Award for Excellence and Innovation in the Arts
- Had its Arts Council funding restored and gained the status of being (from April 2015) a National Portfolio Organisation.

In short, Derby Theatre has changed in a short time from being a 'basket case' to being a highly innovative, entrepreneurial 21st Century creative organisation - through clear, radical vision, strong partnerships and exemplary leadership. And its audiences are growing.

IN CONCLUSION

Sun Tzu wrote in the Art of War: "Plans never survive the first encounter with the enemy" while General Dwight D Eisenhower said, when planning D-Day, the largest military operation in history: "The plan is nothing; planning is everything."

So be flexible. There is no such thing as the perfect plan but you have to do the homework and know the options.

Sue Hoyle, Clore Leadership Programme

Leadership: Creativity & Community

Sue Hoyle of the Clore Leadership Programme explains how the programme came into being and how the arts community in the UK was actively involved in translating a vision into reality. Here she describes how leaders are developed and what she sees as the role of the leader, and the qualities and skills that leaders need. Through a series of practical examples she outlines the different values-led approaches that various leaders in the UK are using to engage audiences and communities.

CHOOSING LEADERSHIP

My view of leadership places values at the heart of an organisation – values which are exemplified in the behaviour, decisions and actions of the leader, and which determine the culture of that organisation and the way in which it connects with its audience and other stakeholders.

But first, I need to explain my own view on what a creative leader is, and also what we mean by 'audience-centric'. Clore Leadership doesn't produce an artistic programme, and it doesn't possess an 'audience' in conventional terms. How, then, can our own practice set an example for creative leadership in audience-centric organisations?

The first part of that answer lies in my view of what leadership itself means. In my definition, leaders could include, for example, artistic and executive directors of performing arts organisations; heads of marketing, communications, production and development; musicians, choreographers, artists and designers; heads of culture for local government; and board members – in order words, people in the centre of organisations as well as at the top, people who are outside organisations as well as those within. Leadership is about activity, behaviour and relationships, not simply status, position or a job title. Leadership is not something you are given – it is something you choose, because you want to make a difference to - and through - culture. The key thing is that leaders are change-makers: making change demands an appetite to create, and so, in that sense, all successful leaders are creative.

Secondly, for me 'audience-centric' means, at its core, paying attention to the needs, desires and development of others, whether it is the culture we consume or the opportunities we create. Contemporary British society is changing rapidly: for example, 30% of the population us under 25; fewer than half of the population of London identifies themselves as "white British" (compared to 80% across the country); and around 16% of working age adults in the UK are disabled [1] [2] [3]. Those proportions vary from community to community, but overall, the artistic programming, workforce, audiences and, importantly, the leadership of the arts and culture do not currently reflect the diversity and variety of the people that they serve. Through the Clore Leadership Programme, we look to bring greater diversity into leadership, and do this not just to change the profile of leadership itself, but to make sure that the culture of leadership is truly reflective of audiences – not just the audiences who engage with culture already, but the very different potential audiences who have the right to access culture.

Where does the Clore Leadership Programme come from? In 2002, an independent philanthropic charity, the Clore Duffield Foundation, set up a task group to find out what they could do to help address the leadership "issue". In the UK we had realized that there simply were not enough cultural leaders to go round. Not enough peo-ple were putting themselves forward for these challenging roles, and many of the leaders in the major cultural institutions seemed to have got there by accident, rather than design. The Foundation consulted widely with hundreds upon hundreds of people in (and outside) the arts community across the UK, and concluded that the situation could get worse rather than better unless a new and more diverse generation of leaders could be developed.

Vitally, after this period of consultation, it was the arts community that came up with the solution, and the Foundation that acted upon it. The issue was not about talent. It was about opportunity, networks and readiness to lead. The arts community recommended that a new organisation should be set up, which could actively engage in talent-spotting and fast-tracking potential leaders across the whole cultural sector: the Clore Leadership Programme

We have an open application process and all the courses we run are very practical, not theoretical, and include attachments to organisations outside your comfort zone. The people who take part in our programmes learn through valuing difference – other artistic forms, other models of leadership and engagement, other countries, other cultures. They learn about themselves from other people's experience (including their fellow participants), from self-reflection, from seeing leaders at work, and from trying out things for themselves.

Our approach to leadership development is not just about selecting individuals, it is about making sure that the cultural sector as a whole is supportive of leadership, understands its importance and helps shape the future. It is as much about changing the culture of leadership as the leadership of culture. We are trying to give leaders the skills and perspectives that they need and to help them to be less isolated, to learn from one another and give each other support.

Over the last ten years, we have introduced a number of different leadership initiatives, including a development programme for the Boards of Directors of cultural institutions and for Chairs and Chief Executives working together, and an international partnership in Hong Kong, providing tailored week-long retreats for East Asia's next generation of cultural leaders.

The model for each programming strand is different, according to the local context and the needs, circumstances and working pattern of people – from digital entrepreneurs to archaeologists. In tailoring our programmes to the needs and specific issues affecting our participants, and asking them to help us develop and evolve, Clore is, in my view, a fundamentally audience-centric organisation. Even after ten years, and even with approximately 1700 leaders and 500 Board directors reached through our programmes, the demand remains.

What does this example tell you about engagement with your community (in this case the arts community)? Firstly, when the Clore Duffield Foundation first identified the problem, it was important that the community was actively involved in finding the solution. They gave the idea their backing and – perhaps – it helped that the initiative came from an independent, individualistic (and generous) foundation, rather than a government department. Secondly, the community was involved in delivering the programme – it offered a way of "giving back" as mentors, speakers, facilitators and secondment hosts. It has also involved people choosing to give back financially, since both individual Fellows and cultural organisations are now giving money to support our Fellowships. The arts community feels it has ownership of the Clore Leadership Programme. Third, we never stopped evolving – no-one course we run is like another.

What are the principles and values which under-pin this?

PRINCIPLES AND VALUES OF CREATIVE LEADERSHIP

A. Consistency and constancy

Stay true to your mission. We were set up to strengthen leadership by developing the next generation.

Our focus is on people in their early to mid-careers. We have been tempted to drift into providing leadership refreshment for experienced leaders or delivering programmes across the world. That would dilute what we do best. Many arts organisations deliver the same message – 'less is more'. A small-scale world-class programme can have infinitely more impact than constantly increasing your output. Ambition is about quality, not just scale.

B. Excellence and relevance

Striving to be the best we can be, playing to our strengths and keeping our antennae tuned to what people need and how they rate us - which links to openness; being alert and connected. We endeavour to attract the best leadership talent by working in partnership with locally-based arts organisations that can identify experienced leaders as ambassadors for leadership, and who can act as talent scouts for younger future leaders. Our recent external perceptions analysis told us some home truths about how some people perceive us. We need to strengthen our communications effort to break down perceptions, but we also need to revisit our programmes because some of those perceptions are truths.

C. Curiosity

An interest in what others are doing i.e. peers, competitors and those outside your immediate "sector".

D. Courage

Trying out new things and being prepared to fail. We are constantly fine-tuning the content and structure of our programmes, we are fidgety, we do not stand still, we do not want to fail but we are prepared to risk mistakes in order to get stronger.

E. Trust

The way that we run our activities is based upon mutual trust between us and the arts communities. Clearly, without that trust, openness and preparedness to fail, Clore Leadership would not work.

QUALITIES OF CREATIVE LEADERS

Given the demands on cultural leaders, it would be naïve to think that it is all about values and principles. Values get you buy-in and loyalty from those who work closely with you, but equally critical are the qualities and skills that enable talented individuals to translate their vision and values into strategy and action, attracting the support of a necessarily wide range of stakeholders.

Which, therefore, are the critical qualities and skills that leaders need?

- **Resilience** and staying alert in today's fast changing, fluid world
- **Openness** to ways of making and engaging with culture that we cannot yet imagine
- **An ability to thrive on uncertainty** and complexity, trust their own judgment, to take difficult decisions and face up to risk rather than run away from it
- **Not fearful** of the unknown
- **Entrepreneurial**, flexible and able to respond to opportunities. To borrow an image from Farooq Chaudhry, producer of Akram Khan Company: leaders should be like bamboo. They may bend in the breeze but they never break. In other words, they stay true to their mission
- **Collaborative**, striving to extend their networks, building alliances and working in partnership with others
- Able see the **big picture**, across and beyond culture.

In summation, I am talking about leaders who are excellent navigators, with a clear sense of artistic mission and social purpose, and the ability to plan strategically by keeping an eye on the horizon as well as having their antennae tuned to what's around them – leaders who have a heart of gold and nerves of steel.

'Hard' Leadership skills

I believe that leaders never stop learning and constantly need to refresh their skills, perspectives and networks. I have talked about the "soft" qualities, but what are the hard skills that leaders need today? Feedback from the leaders who do our programmes tells us that they need:

- **Financial management** – you do not have to be an accountant but you need to be able to ask the right questions of accountants; you need to be able to talk convincingly, with authority and knowledge, about your financial profile and needs. If you do not know about money, you will trip up
- **Strategic planning** – it is one thing to talk about the vision on the horizon, but quite another to work out the route to get there, otherwise you will get lost and distracted
- **Fundraising** – an imaginative approach to building relationships and knowing when and how to make the 'ask'. Effective leaders do not leave fundraising to others – you are the best person to tell the narrative
- **Advocacy skills** which you can adapt to different audiences and circumstances
- **Negotiation skills**, as well as internal and external communication skills
- **Digital literacy**
- **Working with Boards**

- **Knowledge and understanding of politics** – being an operator, a civic player.

Currently, the applied skills which leaders are demanding, and which Clore Leadership gives them through follow up workshops, include handling partnerships and mergers, managing change and having difficult conversations.

Not all of these skills have to be found in the same degree in one person. There will be different strengths across the team and of course everyone should be encouraged to play to their strengths, but effective leaders combine passionate dedication to artistic mission, with values, leadership qualities and the essential skills that I have just listed. You are vulnerable without them.

CREATIVE LEADERSHIP IN ACTION

What does this kind of leadership look like in action? I have talked about us, about Clore Leadership, but I also want to give a few examples of inspiring creative leadership in audience-centric organisations in the UK, from individuals who embody the values and skills that I have just mentioned.

When Kerry Michael took over as Artistic Director of Theatre Royal Stratford East in 2004, he recognized that for the theatre to sustain its im-portance and credibility in an immensely diverse and rapidly changing part of London, it had to truly listen to the community of which it is a part. Kerry made it his mission to bring London's new communities to the stage, portraying their experiences, for example of second and third generation immigrants, and in 2012 made history by having the first British Black musical transfer to the West End. In addition, the theatre's Open Stage project invited the community to programme and curate Theatre Royal Stratford East for six months in the run up to the London Olympics. Radical and ambitious, Open Stage was one of the biggest mass-consultation and community curating projects of any theatre in the UK.

The project grasped the fact that art and culture itself doesn't stand still. Digital technology has disrupted the way in which art is created and engaged with. Audiences have become makers and producers, not simply consumers, and arts buildings are no longer venues where people passively receive performances or observe exhibitions - they are social spaces where creativity, dialogue, and exchange take place. This is the driving ethos behind one of the UK's newest and most exciting cultural venues – Cast in Doncaster, an otherwise culturally deprived town. Director and Clore Fellow Kully Thiarai says that Cast's "vision is about trying to make this the cultural living room for the town – both physically and metaphorically" [4]. The organisation's impressive visitor numbers and blossoming profile demonstrates how embedded audience-driven programming can successfully buck the trend in a decline of cultural provision for the UK's regions. As Kully states, in the case of the people of Doncaster, it's not a lack of aspiration, it's just a lack of experience.

Both Kerry and Kully understand that heading up an arts organisation goes beyond cultural leadership, it demands civic leadership too, and responsibilities that go way beyond one's remit or job title. Above all, it demands producing art that is reflective of the society of which it is a part. We now recognize that culture can make a significant contribution to the economy, to social cohesion and well-being, to health and to education, and we are starting to gather together the evidence to prove it. This means that cultural leaders need to recognise that making the case for culture is an essential part of their responsibilities.

I chose Cast and Theatre Royal Stratford East because they jumped into my head so easily, and that is because of the clarity of their mission. Communities 'get it' and feel part of its evolution. Another UK organisation, the National Theatre of Wales, counters a lack of a permanent building and a tiny staff team with a similarly powerful mission statement:

"The nation of Wales is our stage: from forests to beaches, from aircraft hangers to post-industrial towns, from village halls to nightclubs. Bringing together storytelling poets, visual visionaries and inventors of ideas, National Theatre Wales collaborates with artists, audiences, communities and companies to create theatre in the English language, rooted in Wales, with an international reach. You'll find us around the corner, across the mountain and in your digital backyard [5]."

Beautifully crafted words like these simultaneously convey the organisation's artistic identity and community roots.

Some Clore Fellows like Matt Peacock have committed themselves to redressing the balance between art and communities, by working with groups that were previously denied a cultural offer. Matt's organisation, Streetwise Opera, brings together homeless people and professional opera singers to create high quality productions, and initiated an event called "With One Voice", hosted by the Royal Opera House in London in 2012. This was unprecedented – the first time in history that an event for homeless people was included in the Olympic celebrations. It brought together over 300 people with experience of homelessness from across the UK and helped start the first global network of arts and homeless organisations. Matt has been invited to work with communities in Brazil in advance of the 2016 Olympics and is visiting Tokyo in February to talk about how homeless people can be involved in the 2020 Olympics.

CONCLUSIONS

We can perhaps learn from one another, and from those working in other areas of culture. I want to finish with an example from a Clore Fellow, and one which embodies all of the creative leadership qualities and behaviours that I have been discussing. Tony Butler's Happy Museum Project is a pioneer for recognising museums' roles in community wellbeing and renewal. It awards funding to regional museums, of all sizes, to develop their community practice, fosters peer research and leads advocacy initiatives on museum community leadership. The project takes a view of sustainability, which looks beyond financial and resource management, and considers a museum's role as steward of people, place and planet, supporting institutional and community resilience in the face of global financial and environmental challenges. It's not worthy but fun: Woodhorn, a rural mining museum, has a resident comedian, whilst Manchester Museum has a project taking play as its theme.

In creating the Happy Museum network, Tony bridges the illusionary divide between cultural and civic leadership, and shows that successful creative leadership involves empow-erment of others; the Happy Museum fosters citizen curators, it enables communities and cultural organisations to shape their own opportunities according to their needs. Leadership is all about people: today's creative leaders don't think of audiences as them and us – they talk about 'we'.

As leaders, we need to trust the next generation and develop them. We might not understand all of the opportunities and possibilities that there are for engagement – but tomorrow's cultural leaders will.

REFERENCES AND FURTHER READING

[1] Index Mundi (accessed on 20/1/2/14). **United Kingdom Age Structure**. [webpage] Available: http://www.indexmundi.com/united_ kingdom/age_structure.html

[2] Peter Bazalgette. (accessed on: 20/12/14). **Arts Council and the Creative Case for Diversity**. [PDF]. Available: http://www.artscouncil.org.uk/media/ uploads/Sir-Peter-Bazalgette_Creative-Case-speech_8-Dec-2014.pdf

[3] Office for Disability Issues. (accessed on 21/12/14). **Disability Facts and Figures** [webpage]. Available: https://www.gov.uk/government/publ ications/disability-facts-and-figures/disability-facts-and-figures

PART III

Elements Of A Culture.Shift

Benita Lipps

Elements of a Successful Culture.Shift

In the third part of this publication, we'll be looking at some of the key building blocks of a successful audience development strategy:

1) communication,
2) outreach and community building
3) civic engagement,
4) audience education,
5) artistic co-creation
6) creating a learning organisation

It may be interesting to point out that there's a certain logic to the order in which these case studies are presented:

The **intensity of the interaction** between theatres and audiences increases from making connections via dialogue to – ultimately – collaboration and co-creation.

The **ownership** of creative and aesthetic output gradually shifts from the performing arts organisations towards the audiences. While communication and engagement are mainly directed by the houses themselves, artistic co-creation and audience-centric leadership require audiences as a partner.

Consequently, the **level of strategic leadership** required, and the **impact** on the core of the organisation increases. A good communication strategy does not necessarily affect the creative direction of an organisation; co-creating new work with the audience certainly does.

While this list is by no means conclusive, it does feature some of the important areas that need to be addressed on the way to becoming an audience-centric organisation. These have been identified by some of Europe's prominent performing arts organisations as areas of strategic importance in their development – and it is their voices that will be heard in this section:

1) AUDIENCE COMMUNICATION AS A STRATEGIC DIALOGUE: DESINGEL INTERNATIONAL ARTS CAMPUS (BE)

This section begins with an article on more audience-centric communication. Evidently, this means using the new (digital) tools and channels to provide more targeted and engaging information. However, this article also shows why it may be worth to elevate the position of communication from an operations to a strategic level. Some may worry that investing too much in marketing 'gimmicks' may take the focus away from the artistic content. Yet good, strategic communication is simply about paying closer attention to the audience, about creating an honest dialogue that the entire organisation – not just the marketing department – can benefit from.

As discussed in the first section of this publication, it is no longer enough to talk at potential audiences. For people to become interested in the work of a performing arts house, they need to know that their input is both needed and appreciated. This starts with transforming a one-way marketing channel into a two-way dialogue. Ideally, it can go as far as creating "loyal fans", or even "evangelists" that will become promoters and disseminators in their own right. That's exactly what deSingel has been doing for the last few years – led by example by their general director. In the first article in this section – **Interlinking arts and audiences** – Jerry Aerts, deSingel's general director for artistic policy, shares some of their best practice on proactive and personalised communication. He reminds us that we need to start with a strong vision, and then ensure to create a dialogue about this vision using today's ever-evolving, tailored channels.

2) OUTREACH AND COMMUNITY BUILDING: YOUNG VIC THEATRE (UK)

Establishing a meaningful, two-way dialogue with audiences and communities is an important step towards strategic audience development, however it is not the only one. As helpful as the communication tools and channels may be to enrich or 'deepen' the audience's experience, communication alone won't suffice it comes to broadening, or diversifying audiences (see section 1 of this book for more on the three activities of audience development). It will be necessary to leave the confines of the theatre in order to engage with community members in their environment, and on their terms. To quote Dragan Klaic: "For a lasting impact, a theatre company or group needs to venture to the city neighbourhoods where ethnic and cultural minorities live, in cooperation with and with the support of local community organisations that can provide a point of entry, lend networks and credibility."1

In the second article of this section – **Our Beating Heart: Creating Community** – Lily Einhorn, Two Boroughs Projects Manager at Young Vic Theatre Company, describes how the Young Vic has made it its mission to create encounters with every inhabitant in their area. Using the example of their 2015 production of 'Happy Days', she shows how community work can be closely interlinked with main stage productions making them an integral part of the artistic output and culture of the theatre. By exploring how the experiences of the play's heroine relate to the lives of real people living and working near the Young Vic, the theatre reaches new groups, attracts new visitors and – most importantly – creates a community of audiences, residents, artists and local groups that enrich the Young Vic as an organisation.

3) CIVIC ENGAGEMENT: DRESDEN STATE THEATRE AND HELLERAU – EUROPEAN CENTRE FOR THE ARTS (DE)

The Young Vic's case study of the 'Happy Days' community project shows that reaching out to one's communities can lead to an enriched – and richer – cultural organisation. When taken to the next level, community engagement will not just benefit the internal culture of the house or create new experiences for community members. It can strengthen and deepen the public debate on issues of key importance to its community. And indeed, strategic audience development aims to drag the performing arts out of the artistic ivory tower and into the public sphere. Out in the real world, arts do have a socio-political role to play. Taking on this civic responsibility can revitalise its standing

and relevance as part of the "broad professional, political and social commitment to public culture as an essential feature of democracy."[ll]

The third article in this section – **Beyond the Stage Door: Let's Get Political** – tells the story of two German theatres that decided to actively participate in a socio-political debate that shook the very foundations of their Dresden home. In late 2014 and early 2015, the city had become the spearhead of the new German anti-immigrant movement 'Patriotic Europeans against the Islamisation of the West' (PEGIDA) – creating an atmosphere of xenophobia, exclusion and intolerance in this 'city of culture'. But, rather than standing on the side-lines, theatre directors Wilfried Schulz (Dresden State Theatre) and Dieter Jaenicke (Hellerau – European Centre for the Arts) decided to jump right into the very centre of the debate.

By becoming political not just on stage, but on the streets of Dresden when joining the battle against PEGIDA, Hellerau and Staatsschauspiel have taken a step beyond community building and towards civic engagement. The article shows how the houses have experienced a new sense of purpose and relevance, transforming from observing cultural institutions, to a pro-active political players in their city.

4) AUDIENCE DEVELOPMENT AND EDUCATION: SADLER'S WELLS (UK)

All contributions so far have shown that an arts organisation and its programmes need to be embedded in its community in order to create a meaningful and lasting relationship between audiences and 'their' houses. Once such a relationship exists, a house can start to develop it further through education and other targeted offers, thus deepening the relationship and broadening the experience of the audience. Most non-commercial performing arts organisations look beyond merely providing amusement to their audience. Instead, they aim to "create meaning – in other words, to meet higher-order emotional needs that help audience to see the world differently, develop an expanded capacity for empathy or gain a deeper self-awareness." III To do so requires audience 'development' in the true sense of the word – educational activities and offers that allow them to further their knowledge and deepen their experience.

An entire field is dedicated to theatres in education, and other contributions in this book touch upon its importance. Taking a slightly different perspective, the fourth article in this section – **Expanding Audience Horizons** – illustrates how Sadler's Wells not only aims to engage their audiences, but to develop their taste and aesthetic horizons: Over the last 10 years, Sadler's Wells has become synonymous with developing innovative dance productions, which not only entertain but challenge and educate its audiences. By programming special events, involving local communities, creating exciting and informal settings, offering affordable entrance fees, and communicating intensively about these activities, Sadler's Wells' audiences are actively encouraged to experience types of dance they might not have seen before.

5) CO-CREATING WITH AUDIENCES: AARHUS TEATER (DK)

No matter how much is invested in education, institutions can only reach new audiences if they create a programme, content and aesthetic that is relevant to the groups they want to reach. One way of producing relevant new programmes without losing one's own artistic mission is to invite members of these new audience groups to actively participate in all aspects of the production, thus becoming co-producers.

The fifth article in this section – **Why We Want Citizens on the Stage** – explains why letting audiences participate in the artistic creation is not just a marketing gimmick, but a strategic artistic decision. It describes how – on a growing number of 'citizen stages' – it's no longer just the actors who create the stories. The artistic team of the theatre is joined by ordinary people in the creation and on the stage, playing the role no one else can play better: themselves.

This new trend can be 'seen as an aesthetic breakthrough and the opportunity to rethink what theatre can be', say authors Anne Zacho Søgaard and Tine Byrdal Jørgensen. Looking at different citizen stages across Europe, their article shows how this approach to audience development can integrate audience development in the creative process. Moreover, it shows that building opportunities for the audience to participate in the production does not have to lead to a 'dumbing down' of the repertoire, nor does it interfere with the need to create and program challenging work – on the contrary. Involving audiences in the creative process can lead to an aesthetic innovation that creates meaningful new connections between the theatre and the surrounding society.

6) CREATING AN AUDIENCE-CENTRIC, LEARNING ORGANISATION: SHEFFIELD THEATRES (UK)

By now it has become clear that strategic audience development cannot be the task of one department alone. On the contrary: audience development has to be located at that creative centre of the organisation. By involving the whole house in the process, performing arts organisation will ultimately change and develop together with their audiences, stakeholders and communities. Strategic and integrative audience development can result in mutual learning on all levels for the organisation and "reflect how a performing arts organisation understands its own character as a public theatre." [IV]

The sixth and final article in this section – **Putting the Public Centre Stage** – shows how improving connections local communities can have a profound and transformative effect on every level of the theatre – from communication via programming to recruitment and strategic management. By moving from predefined workshops and educational formats to flexible, tailor-made opportunities for dialogue, Sheffield Theatres managed to create long-term bonds with its communities. In particular, Sheffield People's Theatre – an intergenerational theatre company made up entirely of non-professional performers from all sections of the city's society – has created a new sense of community. According to its Chief Executive Dan Bates, becoming a more audience-centric organisation has made Sheffield Theatres 'a richer and frankly better organisation'.

Hopefully, this section helps to illustrate the positive effects of audience development on an organisation – effects that go well beyond getting more 'bums on seats'. It aims to inspire creative leaders to take on the adventure of engaging with old and new communities – not once for a special project – but continuously and strategically.

Audience development takes courage and persistency, with experiments, stops, starts, and some downright failures along the way. An audience-centric organisation will be willing to embark on this adventure, keeping up the dialogue with their audiences and looking for inspiration in their communities and through exchanges with their peers. And it will be those audience-centric organisations that are equipped to tackle the changes, transformations and challenges of contemporary society with joy, innovation and creativity.

[i] Dragan Klaic (2012): Resetting the Stage

[ii] ibid.

[iii] Conley in Wallace Foundation (2008): Arts for All. Connecting to New Audiences, p.9

[iv] Dragan Klaic (2012): Resetting the Stage

Interlinking Arts and Audiences

For five years, Antwerp has been the home of a new type of institution: the deSingel international arts campus which manages to not only brings together different art forms, but creates a community with its audience. In this article, Jerry Aerts, deSingel's general director for artistic policy, shares some of their best practice & challenges for truly integrating such a community through proactive & personalised communication. He reminds us that we need to start with a strong vision, and then ensure to communicate them in ever-evolving, new and appropriate channels.

TOWARDS AN INTERACTIVE ARTS CAMPUS

When deSingel opened the new international arts campus building on its existing site in 2010, it was the realisation of a dream conceived almost 150 years before. Peter Benoit, a composer who became director of the Antwerp Flemish Music School in 1867, was a driving force behind the idea that Antwerp should have an institution which was more than just a place for educating students and training artists but a centre where the entire population in the international musical and theatrical scene could interact. Benoit's dream, in which not only the students but also the public at large would have the opportunity to benefit from the range of cultural and artistic activities available, ultimately came true with the creation of the deSingel international arts centre.

"We really needed this new construction and had to fight for over a decade to get the money to construct it," says Jerry Aerts, deSingel's general director for artistic policy. "Now it is not only deSingel as an arts organisation which lives here; there is also a conservatoire – a university for music, theatre and dance for 580

students; there is the architecture institute, there are different resident companies like the ChampdAction ensemble for contemporary music and the international contemporary dance company Eastman (Sidi Larbi Cherkaoui) who share the building we run."

"That's why we changed our name into the International Arts Campus but time doesn't stand still, of course," he adds. "The new idea is that it won't be an arts campus much longer but an arts city – a really vivid community of people who get together in the arts in all different forms."

Every year deSingel organises around 80 music concerts, 120 theatre and dance performances (with ten new creations made in-house), six architecture exhibitions (produced with the Flemish Architecture Institute), and other contextual activities around its programme (lectures, debates, courses, artists meetings with the public).

Bringing the public on campus

Since its inauguration, deSingel's International Arts Campus has been striving to remain true to Benoit's vision while addressing the constantly changing demands regarding audiences that face the arts community in the modern age. The challenge remains to build not just a community of artists, but a community of people.

Community is a strong pillar in the overall construction of this ever-evolving campus. Aerts and his team have been developing new ways of engaging with the public beyond the campus boundaries and the city limits to encourage participation and ownership within deSingel's audience.

That audience loyalty is cultivated through public engagement via deSingel's own printed materials and Web site, a painstakingly constructed network of press contacts and its own social media channels. "We specialise in giving in-depth information to the client; not only in our programme book but also on our web site and in discussions with the audience and students, and gathering the public around the content we're creating," says Aerts. "Communication is something that shouldn't be neglected. If the performance goes no further than the space it is created in, you cannot spread the message so it doesn't reach the public. So for me, it's vital that we open it up as much as possible."

This approach has included making the most of the networks linked to local schools by creating student ambassadors. These are invited onto campus to discuss the theatre's programme, before being set up as active participants in deSingel's ticket-selling scheme. The students not only act as vendors but disseminators of information.

Another initiative involves university students in communications sciences to create short films aimed at attracting the wider public to deSingel's programming which appear on the organisation's Web site.

Ebbing and flowing audiences

The efforts of deSingel to reach new audiences are made complicated by the fact that its audiences are in a state of flux.

"Do you know we lose 30% of our public every year which doesn't come back the next?" says Aerts. "I'm happy with that because we gain 35% every year, so we have a 5% increase. Also, it's a change – there's nothing as boring as always having the same public. They only get older – that's the only thing that happens then. So the challenge is to try and build a loyalty with your public while building a new audience."

"But we also see differences in the public for different art forms," he adds. "One can say that classical music has the most loyal returning visitors, theatre in other languages has the highest flux and dance is somewhere in between. Both new people and returning visitors are important."

"The public is also much broken up into age groups: the oldest and most of those with subscriptions come to classical music; the more exclusive the production is, the more the public is coming from different regions - but this part of the public is not loyal, they just come for the one event they don't want to miss."

Introducing family concerts has also brought in a completely new audience to deSingel. Parents with children (only 35% of these parents were already clients) have become part of its public while grandparents with grandchildren (50% of these grandparents were already clients) have also started to attend.

FROM ENGAGEMENT TO INTEGRATION

Attracting people is one thing, integrating them is something else. For the audience to become part of the fabric of the campus, they need to feel as though they have a voice and that their input is needed and appreciated. Aerts and his team have opened up lines of communication to the public to create a dialogue. "The first thing I do each day is to check the forum or email for any complaints, he says."I don't answer them with an email, I just look in the data system for their home or work number and I call them. I talk to them. I listen to their complaints. The person who wrote an angry email becomes a better client after being talked to and listened to for four minutes. When people are talking positively about your brand, it's very important. It's getting increasingly important. It's not only you who should talk about what you're doing. You need to have a conversation with your audience and maintain that."

The positive responses from the public are compiled and used in deSingel's publicity material, on its Web site and on its social media channels. Comments and short films made from the feedback received run beside the ticketing information of the specific show currently being debated by the public. In this way, the audience's own stories and experiences are promoted and shared.

A clear vision, communicated through ever-changing channels.

"This is the essential part of what we do; creating opportunities for a closer bond between the general public and the artists, to organise as many different things as possible to bring all of this together," says Aerts. "We know more than ever that we have to give visibility to all of that; we need to use all the techniques which are available."

"All of our communication is not only saying what is coming up, but also giving comments, telling stories, as well in printed matter as on website, e-mail or social media. The most important issue is that the client gets the feeling that he is involved in what we are doing, that he can react and is listened to. This will not mean that we automatically will change or programme selection in favour the clients more popular choices. We just want to convince them to be more adventurous, to take some risk together with us next to their more automatic participation to the 'canon' of the arts. The arts campus climate needs to be a shared vision. It must become a vivid arts city, a community where values are shared."

"What we want to promote is real creative communication in the arts sector," he concludes. "I think it's important that we don't stick to the old methods. The communication of deSingel's image and vision is our DNA. Almost every performance, every exhibition must confirm that image. Then there is the programme communication which has the main aim of creating momentum. Momentum which is considered to be important: lots of press coverage, lots of public attention and not only shared by a small community of the inner circle around the theatre. This integrated approach all around the performances and art forms needs to be continued and needs to be changed continuously."

Lily Einhorn, Young Vic Theatre

Our Beating Heart: Creating Community

Turning a Little Further — A Two Boroughs Community Show

The Young Vic theatre in London is situated on the border of two boroughs - Lambeth and Southwark. For many years, it has been exploring, celebrating, and writing a common history with the people of these communities through the Two Boroughs project. The theatre believes that anyone living in these two boroughs should visit the Young Vic at least once in their life. Some may never return, but there's a chance that this first encounter will be the start of a lifelong relationship. In this article Lily Einhorn - Two Boroughs Project Manager – talks about why it's well worth taking this chance.

'Imagine a woman up to her neck'

Samuel Beckett's Happy Days did just that. But where would this woman go if she could move? What would this woman do if she was able to escape from her mound of dirt? Who would this woman be if she was not Winnie?

ENGAGING TWO BOROUGHS

Aiming to strongly anchor the Young Vic in its two geographical neighborhoods, the Two Boroughs Project is open to any resident or community group of Lambeth and Southwark. As well as giving away thousands of free tickets and running workshops and theatre clubs, Two Boroughs, a strand of the Taking Part department which also engages local young people and schools and colleges, stages two community shows per year.

Working with a full professional creative and production team, the shows are put on in one of the Young Vic's three theatre spaces with a cast made up of local individuals and community groups. Each piece is inspired by something the theatre has running concurrently in the main house, so that the shows in Taking Part become integral to the artistic output and culture of the building.

These Happy Days

In February and March 2015, the Young Vic staged a production of Samuel Beckett's Happy Days, directed by Natalie Abrahami. Trapped in a scorched wasteland with her detached husband, the play's heroine Winnie keeps despair at bay with ritual, song and her trusty lipstick. It is a tale of resilience – of one woman's ability to survive against overwhelming odds.

The production felt in many ways like one woman's story - so we wanted to use it as a starting point to tell more stories, of more women. Of women who, like Winnie, find themselves defined by something outside of their control.

The Winnies of Lambeth and Southwark

For each Two Boroughs community show we engage local individuals as well as harder to reach community groups who may not otherwise have the opportunity to participate in such a long and intense project. For this show it felt right to look to women in the community whose experience in some way paralleled Winnie's, so we decided to try to engage some groups of female carers: women who were defined by their choice to

care for others when that meant their world shrank around them. The rubble piled higher. Up to the neck.

We met two groups of unpaid, female carers, one from each of our two boroughs of Lambeth and Southwark. With them we created movement and text that enabled us to imagine freedom and escape, and to describe the daily realities of life for these extraordinary, ordinary women. We watched Happy Days together and discussed it as a group, the carers drawing out parallels with their own lives that we suspected were there, and seeing in Winnie shades of themselves that we would never have considered.

Together We Are Turning a Little Further

Myself and the director, Laura Keefe, travelled to both groups each week for four months. When working with harder to reach groups we understand it is difficult for them to come to us, so we try to make their engagement as simple as possible by taking the sessions to them. It is also a vital gesture: we value them enough to go to them. We kept the sessions short, full of long chats over cups of tea: powered by biscuits and laughter. All of the movement was improvised by the cast, which also included twelve local women who auditioned to be part of a core movement group, in separate sessions led by Coral Messam. The text was generated by exercises led by performance poet Francesca Beard who then wove the writing together into a lyrical ensemble piece. The show was brought together into a joyous whole by Laura on a beautiful set, complete with swings and glitter pool, designed by Fly Davis. The title, Turning a Little Further, was a stage direction from Beckett's text that seemed to fit perfectly. The compulsion to move, just a little more, even when your feet are stuck.

The Story Behind the Story

For the carers, coming to rehearsals every week and juggling their responsibilities with our sessions was an ongoing negotiation. Over the course of the project we got to know these amazing women with an often forgotten role in our society. It is estimated that unpaid carers currently save the UK government £119 billion a year. Almost as much as the entire NHS budget. Their carer's allowance is currently £61.35 per week. The show was staged on the eve of the UK general election which gave power to a Conservative government bent on making welfare cuts to women like them. As a company we all wanted to say something about how carers' lives are affected, daily, by the powerful, but who are invisible except to those relying on them every minute of every hour of every day. Forever. No one knows these women when they walk by in the street.

Staging Joy.

From the start we felt that the sessions themselves needed to be joyful - to be a respite - and we hope we translated that to the stage. The joy in small moments. The power of taking a breath. Dancing. If it is theatre's job to tell the stories of a society, to tell us our stories of ourselves, then we wanted to tell those stories that we do not hear, do not know exist. We did not give anyone a voice, we simply allowed some forgotten voices to be heard. It was a joy and a privilege creating this piece with these women. Every story told on stage was true. Every woman stood with many more behind her. This show was for all those women, keeping the world turning, one day at a time.

CREATING COMMUNITIES

Using a main house show as a starting point enables us at the Young Vic to engage with our local community in a completely new way, taking themes or stories drawn from the production and seeing how those can translate into a particular element of their lives.

Working in this way not only engages new people – often those who have had no previous access to the arts – but it stimulates and enhances the general life of the theatre. These communities become its audience: its beating heart.

At the Young Vic, our audience is a heterogeneous, vibrant collection of individuals and its diversity reflects back towards the stage and reverberates around the building. Creating work with local people and different groups means that collectively we are creating a new form of artistic community around one building – constructing a central space that every person who passes through our door feels an equal part of, whether they are starring in a main house show or taking part in a workshop; a young person or a member of a drug and alcohol rehabilitation programme.

The unique atmosphere that fills each space creates an opportunity for each piece of professional theatre to speak with people it may not ordinarily be able to, and the theatre becomes a stronger whole through the wholehearted embrace of a multitude of experiences in its seats and on its stages. The women of Turning a Little Further thanked us for 'remembering' them, for 'listening'. We can only thank them for participating in one of the most vital theatrical conversations we have ever been a part of. Long may we continue to turn.

© Photos: Helen Murray

Benita Lipps

Beyond the Stage: Let's Get Political

FROM AUDIENCE ENGAGEMENT TO CIVIC ENGAGEMENT

Adorno famously wrote that all art is an uncommitted crime. What he meant was that as an exemplar of free subjective expression, art challenges the status quo by its very nature. In that sense, all art touches the political sphere. And indeed, performances have been known to fire revolutions in the not so distant past – such as the staging of Daniel Auber's La Muette de Portici at Brussel's La Monnaie on the eve of the Belgian revolution. However, in most of today's mainstream theatre, any political challenge tends to play out within the safe confines of the stage, rather than spilling from the auditorium into the surrounding streets. But what happens if a theatre decides to engage not just in the political sphere, but also in everyday politics? Two Dresden theatres are redefining their remit.

From October 2014 to spring 2015, the new German anti-immigrant movement 'Patriotic Europeans against the Islamisation of the West' (PEGIDA) dominated the headlines. The reputation of its birthplace – Dresden – suffered greatly as 'normal citizens' walked the streets in weekly demonstrations against foreigners and their 'bad influence' on German culture. But, rather than accepting Dresden as the new 'capital of xenophobia', theatre directors Wilfried Schulz (Dresden State Theatre) and Dieter Jaenicke (Hellerau – European Centre for the Arts) are using their stages to actively fight for openness, tolerance and democracy in their city.

PEGIDA? WHAT'S PEGIDA?

The 'Patriotic Europeans Against the Islamisation of the West (German: Patriotische Europäer gegen die Islamisierung des Abendlandes)', is a recent German anti-Islam political movement that started in Dresden in October 2014. In weekly demonstrations, participants have been calling for more restrictive immigration laws, particularly for Muslims. Portrayed as the outlet of 'angry citizens' from the centre of society ('Wutbürger' in German), rather than a movement of right-wing extremists and neo-Nazis, PEGIDA has raised concerns about the openness and tolerance of German society.

Participants cite their mistrust in policy makers and the mainstream media, as well as their fear of 'losing their national identity and culture' due to an 'increasing Islamisation' as the main reason for their participation. Often portrayed as a movement of concerned citizens, PEGIDA has undeniable racist tendencies. Offshoots of PEGIDA formed in other German cities and various European countries. Participation in Dresden peaked in January 2015 with up to 20.000 people attending the weekly demonstration. Since then, numbers have decreased to a few thousand by March 2015.[1]

In addition to a concrete fear of increased assaults on Dresden's foreign inhabitants, PEGIDA had a negative impact on the image of the 'cultural city' of Dresden. This translated into increasing cancellations by tourists in early 2015 as well as concerns about the city's application to become the European Capital of Culture in 2025.[II]

Dieter Jaenicke and Wilfried Schulz

ENGAGING WITH POLITICS: DRESDEN'S CULTURAL SCENE

After an initial period of shocked paralysis, many artists and cultural institutions have become active in their stance against PEGIDA: On 22 December 2014, the Semperoper (Saxon State Opera) - right on the movement's demonstration route - turned off its outdoor lighting and projected slogans such as 'refugees welcome' and 'Dresden is for all' on its exterior walls. In early January, more than 20 cultural organisations created the 'Initiative for a Cosmopolitan Dresden' (Initiative for ein Weltoffenes Dresden #WOD). A joint calendar of exhibitions, performances, discussions and other cultural events has been created. Together, the institutions aim to "set a signal for an open society, for tolerance and solidarity - and against fear mongering and populism."[III]

In particular, the two theatre directors leading the #WOD movement - Dieter Jaenecke (European Centre for the Arts Hellerau) and Winfried Schulz (Dresden State Theatre) - have taken on the fight against intolerance and xenophobia in their city: "It is our task as theatre-makers to actively reflect the most pressing and virulent issues of the society we live and work in" explains Dieter Jaenicke.[IV] For Winfried Schulz, it's a question of taking a public stance – together with others actors from politics and civil society: "The boundaries between insensitivity and open xenophobia - even misanthropy - are fluent. This is why we have to set a clear sign for liberalism - in the best sense of the word - in politics, civil society and - of course - in art and culture."[V]

The State Theatre Dresden: Beyond Responsive Programming

Geographically, the State Theatre Dresden is located just off PEGIDA's demonstration route. Those who plan to attend a performance on Monday evenings had to cross a sea of PEGIDA protesters. In the eyes of the theatre, this makes it even more important not to stand by and watch: "We will have to take ownership and work through this issue. Dialogue is a given in our society, it is even more important at the moment to take a clear stance and to preserve the core values of our culture: inclusion, support and caring attention, not differentiation and exclusion." explains Wilfried Schulz.[VI]

The State Theatre Dresden is reflecting the need for dialogue in its 2015 programming. Wilfried Schulz explains: "It is possible to address the phenomenon 'PEGIDA' with the means of art and culture, to reflect on it publicly. That's my task as a theater director in Dresden.[VII] [...] We are now offering a series of events for which we invite people via the Refugee Council."[VIII]

This includes surtitled performances for non-German speaking inhabitants and refugees, discussion evenings, and productions that deal with questions of tolerance, civil society and xenophobia. "We want to set a sign for the openness at the centre of our civic society. We invite these 'foreigners' - that so many people seem to be afraid of - to our performances - to specially selected performances. This establishes a dialogue, because integration is a not a one-way street." explains Wilfried Schulz.[IX]

Moreover, the actors jointly decide to end their performances with the reading of a 'call for tolerance and openness' (Aufruf our Weltoffenheit) - an initiative that has its roots in the protests for German unification in 1989. Reinstating this 'new tradition' has been very well received by the theatre's audience: "It is important, and it has something touching when an audience of 800 people rises from its seats after a performance of 'Brave New World' to applaud [the resolution]. The so-called "other Dresden" is looking for a point of identification, but also for relief from these feelings of powerlessness against a movement that has been gaining ground in this city. There is a need to say: No, what you see on TV is not Dresden. We are the majority - it is PEGIDA - not us - which is 'the other Dresden'" explains Wilfried Schulz.[X]

Radical Internationalization at the European Centre for the Arts Hellerau

In response to PEGIDA, Hellerau has heralded the motto of 'radical internationalization' for its 2015 programme and has decorated its outside walls with banners declaring 'refugees are welcome.'

Concretely, Hellerau aims to address the questions of refugees, xenophobia and tolerance artistically: scheduled productions such as 'Motus / Caliban Cannibal / Interrobang / Pre-enacting Europe' question the notion of a 'fortress Europe'. In addition, Hellerau offers free tickets for asylum seekers - inviting them to actively participate both in the cultural programme and in a dialogue with other audience members. Moreover, the 21 employees in Hellerau have volunteered to become sponsors to selected Roma refugees in Dresden, leading to a large-scale performance project on the situation of Sinti and Roma in September 2015. "Nothing makes more sense than integrating the Roma refugees of Dresden into this project"[XI], says director Dieter Jaenicke.

But interactive programming, free tickets and banners are not the limit of Hellerau's civic engagement: the theatre offered the city of Dresden part of its facilities for the safe accommodation of refugees – with staff volunteering to support these new residents actively: "We do have the space [... and] dealing with people from all cultures is part of our daily practice" says Dieter Jaenicke, explaining the reason for this unusual offer.[XII]

Jaenicke believes that – rather than always trying to understand the fears expressed by PEGIDA members – it's high time to address the fears of foreigners affected by this movement: Hellerau does not want its international artists to worry whether they are safe at night on the way to their hotel – nor do they want any other foreigners to feel molested and vilified on the streets of Dresden.[XIII] Therefore, the house aims to become a place for international dialogue – helping to develop new ideas on how to better integrate asylum seekers in Dresden.

AUDIENCE DEVELOPMENT AS CIVIC ENGAGEMENT?

It is still to early to determine how this new civic engagement influences the artistic work of the two Dresden houses, and what impact it has on their long-term perception by audiences and communities. However, three things have already become quite apparent:

Engaging actively in the socio-political live of the city has brought a new sense of purpose, drive and relevance to the houses and its people. Rather than playing out new visions of society on stage, these can now be tested in the real world: "It is important that we don't just talk, or hang a banner, but that we make concrete offers. confirms Dieter Jaenicke.[XIV]

"The theatre has to become a place for mutual understanding and joint reflection" according to Wilfried Schulz.[XV] And indeed, the perception of the houses and their is changing: from (detached) temples for cultural elites to that of an open and inclusive public space for all – including those on the corners of society. "I believe that theatre and art are bound to certain attitudes and ideas of the Enlightenment. We are automatically on the side of the weak and fugitives," says Wilfried Schulz. The stance against PEGIDA has allowed them to reinforce that approach through concrete action.

While it is still too early to discus the impact of this new type of engagement on the old and new citizens of Dresden, it clearly does have an impact on Dresden politics: Dieter Jaenicke confirms that "In the entire six years {that I've been working in Dresden], I've never been as often and repeatedly called by the city mayors as in recent weeks."[XVI]

[I] Patriotische Europäer gegen die Islamisierung des Abendlandes. In: Wikipedia, Die freie Enzyklopädie. Status: 01/04/2015

[II] Thomas Vieregge: Widerstand gegen PEGIDA. Das andere Dresden zeigt Flagge. In: Die Presse, 16/01/2015

[III] Hellerau Website: #WOD – Initiative für ein weltoffenes Dresden

[IV] Und ewig rollt der Stein – Interview with Wilfried Schulz and Dieter Jaenicke. In: Nachtkritik, 26/01/2015

[V] Wilfried Schulz: Rede zur aktuellen Lage in Dresden gehalten auf Einladung des Presseclubs Dresden am 15. Januar 2015 – Website of the Staatsschauspielhaus Dresden

[VI] ibid.

[VII] Wilfried Schulz: PEGIDA ist eine anti-elitäre Bewegung. In RP Online, 26/01/2015

[VIII] Und ewig rollt der Stein (see above)

[IX] Wilfried Schulz: Rede zur aktuellen Lage in Dresden (see above)

[X] Wilfried Schulz: PEGIDA ist eine anti-
elitäre Bewegung (see above)

[XI] Winfried Schenk: Festspielhaus Hellerau: Belegschaft will Flüchtlinge un-
terbringen und betreuen. In: Menschen
In Dresden, 2/12/2014

[XII] Und ewig rollt der Stein (see above)

[XIII] Dieter Jaenicke: Rede zur Jahreseröff-
nung. Hellerau Website 22/01/2015

[XIV] Und ewig rollt der Stein (see above)

[XV] Wilfried Schulz: Wer ist Pegida? In: Theater
Heute, 03/2015

[XVI] Und ewig rollt der Stein (see above)

Expanding Audience Horizons

A Commitment to Audience Development

When Alistair Spalding was appointed Chief Executive and Artistic Director of Sadler's Wells in 2004, the theatre – the former home of the companies that went on to become The Royal Ballet and Birmingham Royal Ballet – was suffering from financial difficulties and the lack of a clear identity, with audience numbers gradually decreasing. Through a combination of risk-taking, instinctive leaps of faith, a dedication to supporting and producing new work and a commitment to audience development, Sadler's Wells was transformed from a struggling theatre into a financially stable and world-renowned dance house.

One of the major changes that inspired the turnaround was the decision to move away from the previous model of just playing host to travelling companies and for Sadler's Wells to start producing its own shows. Not long after being named Chief Executive and Artistic Director, Mr Spalding appointed the first group of Associate Artists - Akram Khan, the BalletBoyz, Matthew Bourne, Jonzi D, Wayne McGregor and Sidi Larbi Cherkaoui - in a move he has described as "a drawn-in-the-sand mo-

ment", which changed Sadler's Wells from a place where work was presented to one where work was made. During Mr Spalding's decade at the helm, the theatre has helped to bring over 90 new dance works to the stage.

TO ENTERTAIN, EDUCATE AND CHALLENGE

As a result of its commitment to nurturing talent, Sadler's Wells has become synonymous with developing innovative productions, which not only entertain but challenge and educate its audience while keeping ticket prices affordable. In 2013-14, 37% of all tickets sold by the theatre were discounted, and 10% of tickets for most main house performances are priced at £12.

The dance house regularly commissions its 16 Associate Artists to create new work for its stage, which usually attracts large audiences. Recent productions include Russell Maliphant's Still Current – featuring duets and trios integrating qualities and vocabulary from contemporary dance, ballet, martial arts and hip hop – and Sidi Larbi Cherkaoui's m¡longa,

an exploration of the rich world of tango. Both shows are currently touring internationally.

Being able to bring productions back also enables the theatre to grow its audiences, as critical acclaim and word-of-mouth publicity prompt new audiences to go to performances they did not see the first time around.

Sadler's Wells' audiences are actively encouraged to experience types of dance they might not have seen before or engage with thought-provoking work that invites them to consider dance from a different perspective.

One of the dance house's latest audience development-driven projects is Sadler's Sampled, an annual festival presenting world-class artists and productions at low prices. With standing tickets from just £8, spectators can experience performances in a more informal setting and get closer to the action on stage. It works as an introduction to dance for many of the first-time attendees who are attracted by the variety on offer and the affordable entrance fees.

INVOLVING LOCAL COMMUNITIES

Sadler's Wells has also taken inspiration from the communities living around it to produce shows where what's happening on stage reflects the lives of many of those attending. As such, these productions attract audiences from cultural and social groups from around London which are rarely catered for by large arts organisations.

The annual Breakin' Convention festival of hip-hop dance theatre, started in 2004, is one of the most successful of these initiatives. Under the artistic directorship of Jonzi D, a stalwart of the British hip hop scene, the festival takes over the entire theatre building every May bank holiday weekend with performances, workshops, DJs, freestyle sessions and live aerosol art, in an event where the difference between those on stage and those in the audience is minute. The festival's 10th anniversary in 2013 was attended by 4,300 people. Ten new short works were commissioned from British artists for the occasion. Breakin' Convention also hosted its first free Park Jam in Spa Fields, near the theatre, which attracted 2,800 people. Breakin' Convention also toured to 9 UK cities, giving 44 regional hip hop companies and 450 local dancers the opportunity to perform on stage alongside internationally renowned artists.

Wah! Wah! Girls – a British Bollywood musical produced in collaboration with Theatre Royal Stratford East, which ran in 2012 – was created with the huge Asian community in mind. Effectively a call for this under-represented audience to come to the theatre, it was heeded by 33,400 people in London, Cornwall and Leicester.

The Elixir festival is another example of Sadler's Wells breaking new – or in this case, old – ground in its mission to broaden audience horizons. Challenging the belief that a dancer's career should effectively end well before they're 40, the Elixir festival is a celebration of lifelong creativity and the contribution of older artists. The first edition of the biennial festival, held in September last year, attracted over 2,400 people and included performances by internationally renowned artists, former dancers returning to the stage after 20 years or more, and Sadler's Wells' Company of Elders, all of whom are over 60. The festival challenges perceptions of how a dancer's body should look and has proved popular with audiences of all ages.

THE COMMERCIAL/ARTISTIC BALANCING ACT

It hasn't been all been plain sailing though. Having enjoyed five years of continued success, in 2010 Sadler's Wells invested a considerable amount of money in a large-scale production, Shoes, to be presented for an extended run.

A song and dance revue show on the many memories and emotions people associate with footwear written by Richard Thomas, composer for

Jerry Springer: The Opera, the production was expected to be a huge hit. However, Shoes did not do as well as expected at the box office and this, combined with the effects of the economic recession at the time, negatively affected the theatre's financial performance that year. The experience taught Mr Spalding and his team two things: that there is a time to take risks and a financial crisis may not be one of them; and that Sadler's Wells should stick with what it does best and not try to compete with big commercial West End musicals that have budgets eight times as large.

That said, the experience has not prevented Sadler's Wells from providing its public with more productions holding wide appeal. As well as providing edgy and ambitious new experiences to expand its audience's tastes and minds, Sadler's Wells also brings glamorous, fun-filled performances to its stages in an effort to give its public the widest variety of choice.

Acclaimed choreographer Matthew Bourne's shows are always extremely popular among Sadler's Wells' audiences: over 93,600 people saw New Adventures' new production of Swan Lake in 2013-14, with the theatre reaching 97% capacity.

Today, the theatre continues to successfully perform the balancing act of presenting a number of popular shows to keep the box office healthy, while at the same time retaining its ability to support the creation of inspiring, experimental work. . With 74.5% of its annual income coming from ticket sales at Sadler's Wells and its West End venue The Peacock theatre, – the rest coming from commercial activity and private and public funding (the latter representing only 9% of income) – the dance house knows its audience is its biggest stakeholder and, as such, pleasing them is vitally important.

Through the combination of a solid business model and a varied programme, the organisation is at once ensuring its long-term sustainability and its ability to take a reasonable amount of risk in commissioning, producing and co-producing cutting-edge, original work. It is in this way that Sadler's Wells continues to keep loyal attendees returning for unique experiences while attracting new and diverse audiences.

Anne Zacho Søgaard and Tine Byrdal Jørgensen, Aarhus Teater

Why We Want Citizens On The Stage

"All the world's a stage" according to Shakespeare. Andy Warhol gave it a modern twist with his famous quote: "In the future, everyone will be world-famous for 15 minutes." Several theatres have drawn on this philosophy and are putting ordinary people on the stage to create new synergies between the theatre and its surrounding society.

REALITY IS IN

At Teater Republique you can watch a group of youngsters who are not trained actors, as they talk about their own life experiences as young people, their personal dreams, fears and doubts. At Aarhus Teater, ten people from East Jutland meet up to find out whose life had the most in common with Kafka's fictional character Josef K. At Aalborg Teater, five people from North Jutland share their own personal experiences with death. At Teatru-spalatorie in Moldova, three gay men and three relatives recount the consequences of coming out in a country where being open about your sexuality is life threatening. At Ro Theater in Rotterdam, ten mothers from different ethnic backgrounds reveal intimate details about menstruation, giving birth, to parting from their mothers – while they cook a meal on the stage.

At all of these theatres, reality is the 'in thing'. In fact, reality has been in for the last 20 years but what is new is that it is not just the actors who create the stories, excite the minds and touch the hearts of the audience. Now it is ordinary people on the stage, playing the role of ... well, themselves. They are "everyday experts" - people with first-hand experience in relation to the performance's subject. But what will we actually do with everyday experts on the stage? Is this strictly an audience development and the Artistic Directors' reaction to

a tough competitive situation? Is it just another example of the idea that theatre institutions should be rooted in a democratic society and meet citizens on an equal footing, while being socially responsible and demonstrating diversity on several levels? Or is it an aesthetic breakthrough and the opportunity to rethink what theatre can be? We think it is the latter.

AUDIENCE & AESTHETIC DEVELOPMENT

There are many questions and even more answers. One thing is certain – nothing is black or white and the growth in citizen productions requires a nuanced debate. At the heart of the debate lies the question: to what degree do the pressing needs of the theatre in attracting new audience groups to ensure it has a future go hand in hand with the visions for developing new aesthetic forms? Involving ordinary people in the theatre has inflamed a burning and highly topical cultural and political debate in a new way: If we play the audience development card, have we thrown away aesthetic integrity in a mad hunt for a broad appeal that will attract more people?

Using everyday experts on stage is not something new in Danish theatres but should be seen as being part of a longer development. However, the number of citizen productions has increased significantly in 2014 and both Aarhus Teater and Aalborg Teater have citizen stages, which are dedicated to performances using everyday experts. The future will bring more people onto the stage in Denmark and Warhol can rejoice in his heaven that his prophecy is spreading across Europe. Like every new genre before it, the establishment of citizen stages is being met with equal amounts of excitement and healthy scepticism. Many people are worried that amateurism will infiltrate the Beautiful Art.

However, it would be a fatal error to equate the use of everyday experts with amateur theatre when we talk about which philosophy of art the establishment of citizen stages expresses. On these stages, citizens will not master the art of inhabiting a fictitious role in a storytelling drama – they will not bring a Hamlet or a Jeppe to life in front of an audience. The everyday expert's expertise – the person's strength and vulnerability is that they have their own life invested in the performance's theme. It is exactly this situation that will move us in the audience. As when, in an interpretation of Kafka's "The Trial" at

Aarhus Teater, ten people from East Jutland will soon stand on the stage and with vulnerable defiance, share their own deeply personal experiences with the system for better or worse. The aim of the performance is to get the audience to think about the way the welfare state is organised through a meeting between the theatre's sensory world and the struggles of reality.

It is no secret that citizen stages are conceived as part of an audience development strategy; the growth in citizen stages is the result of the European collaboration project Theatron, an international audience development project supported by the EU and of which Aarhus Teater is a co-founder. However, it would be a little like going into "automatic pilot mode" if one was to conclude that the theatres are trying to gain favour with audiences and their grantors. Audience development and aesthetic innovation are not opposites; on the contrary they are often mutually connected. Admittedly, there may be a reason that the theatre's audience is a relatively homogeneous group of people with more or less the same skin colour and education and income levels that in no way whatsoever reflect society's diversity. A responsible Artistic Director is therefore forced to think about audience development if the theatre's considerable levels of financial subsidy are to be justified. From that perspective, citizen stages have become another aspect of audience development.

Bürger Bühnen Festival

A German-European Theatre Festival

The modern citizen stages originated in Dresden in Germany six years ago and since then, more and more theatres in Denmark and Europe have embraced the concept. More than 1,200 people from Dresden have participated in performances at Staatsschauspiel since the citizen stage was established. It is proof of a theatre success story, which has created a new contract with the city it is rooted in.

This asks the next pressing question concerning the use of citizen's personal stories on the stage. Is this simply the theatre's answer to reality television in the fierce battle for audiences? Through the medium of television we can see "uncensored" breakups, heavily indebted people trapped by unsustainable consumerism, homes that are transformed from wrecks to palaces – the list is endless. The question is whether citizen productions are reality theatre, which is neither interesting nor legitimate. Those theatre professionals who get involved in this form of theatre today, often do so because they genuinely want to revitalise the theatre. Because they ask openly which figures and which voices should we be able to see and hear up on the stage. Of course replacing actors with citizens on the stage who play themselves is a radical measure. It shakes the very foundations of our understanding of what theatre is or can be. But it has always been audacious people who drive the art forward and into new experiments; people with equal measures of delusions of grandeur and sensitivity to the world's development, who have attempted to reshape the foundation of art. Once upon a time the stage was only for actors but someone took a citizen, called that person an everyday expert and put him or her on the stage. A new genre was created and we christened this bastard child "reality theatre". Still not out of the delivery room, those of us who create theatre with everyday experts, are attempting to gesticulate with critics and shout out that this is not an attempt to throw the baby out with the bathwater. Because citizen stages must be seen as being part of a bigger repertoire. Over time in Germany, citizen stages have become a natural part of the repertoire of many of the larger state-funded theatres, exactly the same way as classical plays, family performances, new drama and experimental theatre are part of their repertoire.

HABERMAS ON THE CITIZEN STAGE

When they are strongest, productions using everyday experts can help us to rethink the relationship between the theatre and the public. Citizen stages have something of the German philosopher Habermas' ideal of the 'bourgeois public sphere'. His well-known thesis is that a well-functioning democracy requires public debate, where citizens come together as a public and debate the structure of society and by voicing their opinions they become active partners and opponents of the rules laid down by the authorities. Habermas maintains the public sphere emerged in Vienna, London and Paris at the end of the 18th century, where society's contemporary elite met in coffee houses and as a group discussed the issues of the day. According to Habermas, it followed that the emergence of the public arts institutions up through the 18th and 19th century contributed to the promotion of a critical debate. Even though dramatic changes to the political, cultural and media landscape have taken place since Habermas wrote about the importance of public debate in a democracy, his ideas still provide much food for thought when dealing with the challenges of today.

As an art form theatre has a peculiar characteristic – people meet and assemble to enjoy an intimate theatrical evening and become a single group sharing the same experience. In other words, the theatre allows the opportunity of a face-to-face exchange. It is precisely this face-to-face meeting that makes productions using everyday experts so intense. All else being equal in the stage-audience relationship, it makes a difference that it is citizens up there on the stage who are sharing their real experiences. The meeting between the citizen on the stage and the public represented by the audience is placed in an artistic framework, which organises what is experienced under a logic that immediately looks like "reality" and at the same time perceives reality through art's twisted gaze.

While reality and the theatre partner dance, the evening that is shared in the theatre becomes in an idiosyncratic way an event, where we as the audience are made to reflect over our own position both as citizens and people. And we are in an (almost) exemplary way back with Habermas' visions for the relationship between art and the public. This does not mean that the objective of citizen productions is to create consensus-seeking solidarity in an attempt to legitimise theatre's potential for being useful to the community. No, as the audience we can either identify with the actions and choices that the citizen on the stage has taken or we can disagree with them. Regardless of the aesthetic struggle with one another's point of view and their life choices, the individual in the audience can broaden their understanding to include other people, and we can reflect on society's connectedness and responsibility.

A DIFFERENT AESTHETIC

If we step back a little from the current buzzwords about theatre being rooted in reality and look at the aesthetic produced by the use of everyday experts, so it is precisely when we talk about art, the special aesthetic experience, which will shake up the way we look at the world. Art experience works in other ways than for example, a letter to the editor. When we invite citizens onto the stage, of course it creates another aesthetic. They move differently with a body that bears the marks of an individual life and they deliver text differently than actors. As the audience, we are perhaps moved by the mistakes or the courage and vulnerability of the person who stands on the stage. It creates a special feeling of authenticity. The artistic team works with these parameters in the production and they are put in to move, excite, offend and shock the audience and thus lead them to the above-mentioned reflection.

At Aarhus Teater, the Theatron project has recently received the results from an audience survey, which has allowed us to measure the effect of our citizen stage efforts. In line with the Dresden playhouse, the results show that many people in the audience for our first citizens' performance were new to the theatre or were people who seldom visited Aarhus Teater. This was a direct consequence of the citizens we had found during the outreach work, who had brought their network into the theatre, people who you could clearly tell (and to put it a little harshly) moved in environments that teams of actors did not. Alongside the theatre's normal marketing strategies, we can also use citizen productions to add the old-fashioned word-of-mouth method, which in this case proved to have a surprisingly large effect. The obvious question is, how can the theatre ensure loyalty among these new audience groups? This is the challenge for the future and something that we at Aarhus Teater are focusing on.

INVESTING IN THE THEATRE'S FUTURE

It can sound great, but citizen stages are an investment in the theatre's future – both in relation to developing new aesthetic forms and new audience groups. Now, it is not the case that you can simply take the Dresden model and transfer it directly to another city; each city is different and requires specific cultural efforts. A citizen stage requires a huge amount of outreach work, when you have to find the right people and stories for a performance. It requires artists who have the ability to move around the city's different environments or among the general public – with a certain degree of humility to ensure that there is a real exchange between theatre and city. For every new production and performance theme, a citizen stage will through outreach work meet new groups in society and make space for new voices on the stage. Voices that call out to new audiences, voices that use life's living archive of wisdom based on real experience. Tightly orchestrated around these citizen's voices is the potential to revitalise theatre's expression and leave an echo of the aesthetic's primitive objective; that the aesthetic experience leads the audience to new insights into our shared world. Only in the dialectic between audience development and aesthetic innovation can citizen stages become pulsating art that creates a life-giving stream between the theatre and the surrounding society.

Dan Bates, Sheffield Theatres

Putting The Public Centre Stage

WORKING WITH COMMUNITIES

The best run theatres - the theatres with the most exciting programmes - are those that throw open their doors to communities and make them part of their work. The effect can be energising, galvanising and inspiring for all those involved.

At Sheffield Theatres, improving links with the surrounding communities has had such an effect at every level. It has changed the attitudes of the staff; it has also caused the organisation to 'relax' a little – to become less corporate and it has meant that our theatre doors feel very open.

Working with communities has also improved the theatres' sustainability by growing and developing audiences. This is a great advantage to the business – our audience attendances are growing year on year and our funders recognise that we are connected in a meaningful way with the communities we serve.

Over the last five years, we have continuously improved our approach to working with our communities and there are a number of initiatives that have proved to be particularly successful.

Hands-on workshops

Daniel Evans, the artistic director at Sheffield Theatres leads the Learning programme. Over the last five years he has refined the organisation's offer to move away from a traditional approach to workshops. We now take a more flexible approach, offering bespoke, tailor-made opportunities. These are focussed on skills development and offer experiences for audiences to engage with creative professionals.

Sheffield Theatres run large scale workshops, bringing members of the public into the creative space where they meet with the cast and directors on a production who give a greater insight in to their work.

A programme of workshops has also been developed which enables the participants to work with visiting creative teams, including sessions with a voice coach, singing with the artistic director, stage fighting and most recently, to link with the production of Anything Goes, a tap dancing workshop. One participant, a local business man came out of this particularly gruelling workshop and said it was "the best day of his life". We encourage - and contract - all creative staff to undertake these workshops because this work is vitally important to us.

Sheffield Theatres also run Play Reading Workshops for both adults and children, which follow a format close to the 'book club' concept - the play is read by the group, then discussed and debated. The plays range from new commissions and existing plays to work-in-development.

Over the course of the last year we have hosted the workshop programme has attracted over 6,000 participants, and over 130 workshops.

Reaching out to schools

In the UK, every schoolchild has to undertake some work experience. At Sheffield Theatres we pride ourselves on offering a different kind of experience. Students enjoy a week-long course that includes a series of seminars from the staff. Everyone from the CEO through to finance, press, and production give the students an insight into their roles, the skills required and the budgets we're working with.

Each work experience pupil undertakes a shift working backstage or front of house which gives them a comprehensive understanding of the work on offer. At the end of the week, the pupils create a response to

their consolidated learning. One group created a video, where they started off as 'zombies' non communicating, on their phone, badly dressed, and then went to see a play, and when they left the theatre, they were transformed.

One participant joined the work experience course as she wanted to become an actor. The insight she received during the week made her reconsider and over the years since she has been involved in stage management at the Sheffield People's Theatre and has now enrolled at the Welsh College on a stage management course.

Over 25 staff members participate during the work experience week which has now become integrated into Sheffield Theatres' annual schedule. The company plans to expand the opportunities by increasing the number of weeks on offer to pupils every year.

As well as bringing school children into the theatres on work experience to learn about the organisation, Sheffield Theatres has developed an ambassadors programme with schools in the most challenging areas of Sheffield. These ambassadors are encouraged to bring their peers to the theatre to see shows, and workshops. While this initiative is still in its infancy, the pilot project has gone well. We plan to grow this scheme and include the student population of the city and the more diverse communities.

Another incentive designed to attract younger audiences comes from the ticket pricing. Young people aged 16 to 26 are offered tickets for £5 for all performances, and everyone can see one of the company's own productions for only £1.00 on the first night of the run (public dress rehearsal). The results have been impressive with audiences queuing from 5.00am on the morning of a public dress rehearsal in some cases.

SHEFFIELD PEOPLE'S THEATRE: OPPORTUNITY AND DIVERSITY

One of the organisation's greatest successes in involving the local community is the Sheffield People's Theatre: an inter-generational theatre company made up entirely of non-professional performers from all sections of the city's society. The age range is 12 to 60+ and no one is excluded; one participant performed on stage at the age of 84. Over 300 people auditioned for the last production with 120 people selected; 90 performers, 10 musicians and 20 people backstage.

When the Sheffield People's Theatre company started in 2012, the entire company was very white and middle class, but over the years, through some very specific recruitment initiatives including holding auditions in community centres and local schools, we have gradually diversified the company with 20% now coming from a non-white background and we've had a couple of disabled people join us this year too.

It is a huge commitment for the participants, with the usual duration of involvement lasting for over four months. Many juggle their theatrical roles with day jobs and families and the cast and crew feature people from all walks of life; teachers, surgeons, cleaners, and even a boxer have been involved since the theatre began.

You could ask why they do it. We've found that many people's number one priority is to work in a professional theatre environment. Others want to improve their own skills and most want to meet new people, to try something new and build their confidence. The opportunity to work with people of all ages is a strong motivator and the productions always create a real 'family' bond between the entire company.

All the company are treated as professionals; they are asked to sign a contract that clarifies their commitment to the project and the expectations of the theatre, and the organisers ensure they are treated the same as any professional company working in the theatre.

One area we have learnt from over the years is the huge sense of loss at the end of the show and we ensure that once the company has been formed, there is lots of continual contact with the members. They are invited to special events, to workshops and to engage with the work. They have their own Facebook group and arrange re-unions regularly. I am sure it won't be long until we have our first marriage!

The most recent project the People's Theatre undertook was The Sheffield Mysteries where the group took the traditional creation story, contemporised it and set in Sheffield. The professional creative team was led by artistic director Daniel Evans, who directed the production – which was extremely well received with over 3,000 people attending over the four performances.

The national press are invited to see performances by the People's Theatre, a further demonstration of the professional treatment afforded the group. Both the Daily Telegraph, the Daily Mail came to see The Sheffield Mysteries, and while the reviewers did not really like the script, they both commented on the quality of the production.

Quentin Letts wrote in the Daily Mail: "Amateur Community productions can be a mixture of classic writing and terrible acting. The Sheffield Mysteries is the opposite. The cast of 91 local people, or all ages, is admirable".

The Sheffield People's Theatre, as a project, has also gained national attention. Profiling the initiative, The Guardian wrote: "It's the measure of a thriving regional theatre that it can follow prestige events such as an Othello featuring The Wire stars Clarke Peters and Dominic West with a mammoth community play whose production standards are every bit as impressive".

The next People's Theatre offering - Camelot: The Shining City – is scheduled for July this year and it will prove to be the toughest test yet. The production, which is loosely based on the King Arthur story, will start in Sheffield's iconic Crucible theatre before the audience moves to two outdoor spaces in the city to watch the remainder of the show.

The audience will all have their own headsets and receivers, and the cast will all have radio microphones. This is a radical departure from the norm for the Sheffield People's Theatre and those involved will face new challenges and will need to hone their skills to work outside of the theatre. Slung Low, a theatre company based in Leeds, who are experts in their field of using this technology and site-specific work, are partnered with the People's Theatre on this project to provide the logistics necessary.

The People's Theatre not only gives members of the public an opportunity to act in community shows but also to try their hand at professional productions. Members who have performed with the People's Theatre are sometimes invited to join the cast of shows such as The Winter's Tale as villagers or as children in Oliver! In 2014, 147 Sheffield People's Theatre members were involved in other shows. People's Theatre members now also work for the wider Sheffield Theatres organisation, with several working part-time in the bars, the café, the workshop and the box office.

Sheffield People's Theatre has really galvanised our engagement with the communities around Sheffield and has made us a richer and frankly better organisation. The work we undertook to recruit more diverse participants is now become embedded in our policies and procedures for recruitment for jobs at the theatre - again helping us to diversify our workforce. The same process is being undertaken by our marketing and communications teams.

THE POWER TO CHANGE LIVES

At Sheffield Theatres we believe that the power of theatre can change people's lives and by creating opportunities such as the Sheffield People's Theatre, I feel we are achieving this.

We know that the skills development programme has changed people's lives, as participants are now in full time further education, have changed their career path, and raised their ambitions. We have grown our audiences and we know that the Sheffield People's Theatre members have increased their visits to the theatre by 90%. We are slowly reducing the number of single visits each year but this is a long task.

Community inclusion remains at the forefront of all the organisation's work and it plays a huge role in its planning for the future. The current business plan for the next three years in Sheffield includes increased investment in community development, an increase in the quality of the organisation's work both on and off stage - and in the digital environment, the creation of a programme of free foyer events and the utilisation of the area outside the theatre for free summer performances. All of which will support us in continuing to ensure that the public remain centre stage at Sheffield Theatres.

Lightning Source UK Ltd.
Milton Keynes UK
UKOW01f2154071115

262275UK00012B/126/P